GREAT BATTLES OF THE
CONFEDERACY

GREAT BATTLES OF THE
CONFEDERACY
SWAFFORD JOHNSON

GALLERY BOOKS
An imprint of W.H. Smith Publishers Inc.
112 Madison Avenue
New York, New York 10016

A Bison Book

Published by Gallery Books
A Division of W H Smith Publishers Inc.
112 Madison Avenue
New York, New York 10016

Produced by
Bison Books Corp.
17 Sherwood Place
Greenwich, CT 06830

ISBN 0-8317-3941-X

Printed in Hong Kong

1 2 3 4 5 6 7 8 9 10

Pages 2-3: The forces of
A P Hill arrive to ensure
the Confederate victory
at Antietam.
This page: The ruins of a
Nashville and
Chattanooga Railroad
bridge destroyed during
the Chickamauga
campaign.

CONTENTS

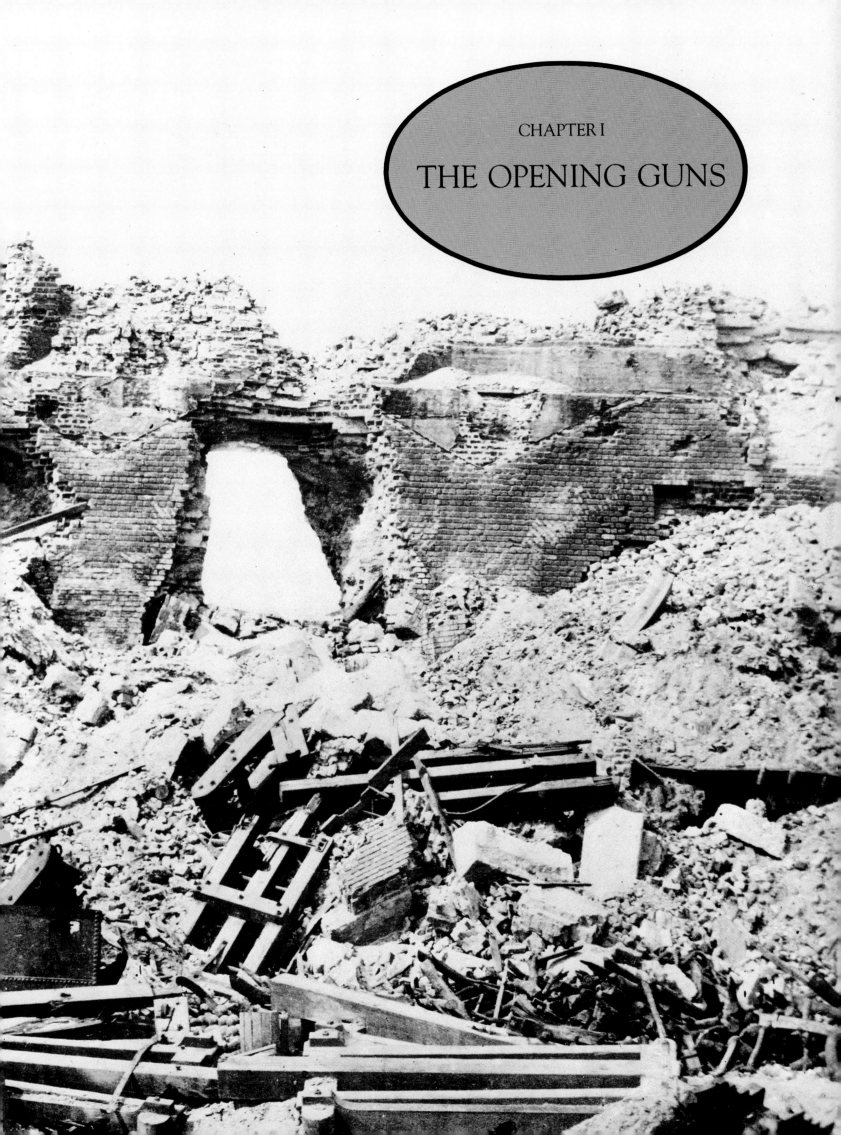

CHAPTER I

THE OPENING GUNS

Previous spread: Fort
Sumter was shelled
repeatedly.

Above: South Carolina,
in a published broadside,
announced its decision to
secede.

Right: Alexander
Stephens (1812-83)
served as Vice-President
of the Confederacy
despite ill health.

On 20 December 1860, a convention of delegates meeting in Charleston, South Carolina, unanimously voted to pass this ordinance:

We, the people of the State of South Carolina, in Convention assembled, do declare and ordain, and it is hereby declared and ordained, that the ordinance adopted by us in Convention, on the 23rd day of May, in the year of our Lord 1788, whereby the Constitution of the United States of America was ratified, and also all Acts and parts of Acts of the General Assembly of this State ratifying the amendments of the said Constitution, are hereby repealed, and that the union now subsiding between South Carolina and other States under the name of the United States of America is hereby dissolved.

It happened at last, the thing long predicted and long feared: the United States, which had fought so fiercely for nationhood and felt themselves to be the hope of the world, were beginning to fall apart. A state had seceded from the Union. Others were ready to follow its lead.

The pressures leading to this secession were many, but underlying them all was the issue of human slavery. By the middle of the nineteenth century that 'terrible institution' had been eliminated from the northern part of the United States as well as from most European countries. In the South, black slavery was an integral part of the region's agrarian economy, most of it based on cotton. But behind the Southern defense of slavery lay more than purely economic concerns. Alexander H Stephens, future Vice-President of the new nation, was to state in a speech of March 1861, that the nation's 'cornerstone rests upon the great truth, that the negro is not equal to the white man.' There was

deep and abiding fear that the slaves were not as contented as they were held to be that if given encouragement they might rise up and slay their white masters. Deeper still was a horror of racial mixing if blacks were given freedom and citizenship (of course, racial mixing actually happened all the time, since many white masters had slave mistresses). Southern fears of Northern abolitionists thus were economic to some extent – slaves were necessary to grow cotton – but even more were emotional. This emotionalism led to furious accusations against the North, most of them fanciful – though there is no doubt that the North planned to contain slavery within the South, not allowing it into new territories in the West, and indeed planned ultimately, somehow, to phase out the institution.

The South had long resented bitterly the North's opposition to slavery and the fierce activism of Northern abolitionists. In its addendum to the ordinance of secession, the South Carolina convention touched on these resentments: 'We affirm that these ends for which [the US] Government was instituted have been defeated, and the Government itself has been destructive of them by the action of the nonslaveholding States. Those States have assumed the right of deciding upon the propriety of our domestic institutions . . . They have encouraged and assisted thousands of our slaves to leave their homes; and . . . have incited [those remaining] to servile insurrection.'

The issues swirling around slavery had, beginning from the inception of the country, tended increasingly to split the nation along sectional lines. Among those corollary issues were the contending doctrines of federalism and of states' rights. Federalism, strongest in the North, proclaimed the primacy of the federal government and its laws; while states' rights doctrine, strongest in the South, upheld the primacy of each state's government and the states' right to nullify Federal laws they did not like – and, in extremity, to sever their bonds with the Union entirely.

Thus over the years two sections of the country pulled apart in economy (the North was more industrialized), in temperament and in culture. On both sides, fear and suspicion gradually supplanted goodwill and reason. Eventually the situation had grown out of control of even the wisest of men. The divisiveness came to a head with the election of Abraham Lincoln, whom the South perceived as a rabid abolitionist. In reality, Lincoln was comparatively a moderate on the issue. He regarded slavery as a great evil, writing at one point, 'If slavery is not wrong, then nothing is wrong.' But Lincoln was willing to go to any lengths to resolve tensions peacefully; if that meant tolerating slavery for the time being, he would tolerate it.

By the time of Lincoln's inauguration on 4 March 1861, he was faced with a rival government of seven Southern states calling themselves the Confederate States of America: South Carolina, Mississippi, Florida, Alabama, Georgia, Louisiana, and Texas. Following the lead of South Carolina, these states had responded to Lincoln's election by seceding from the Union, had drawn up a constitution, appointed a President, and claimed all Federal property within their borders. In his inaugural address Lincoln spoke words of peace: 'We are not enemies, but friends. We must not be enemies. Though passion may have strained, it must not break, our bonds of affection. The mystic cords of memory, stretching from every battlefield and patriot grave to every living heart and hearthstone all over this broad land, will yet swell the chorus of the Union when again touched, as surely they will be, by the better angels of our nature.' At the same time, Lincoln showed himself unalterably opposed to tolerating secession. He would not go to war over slavery, he said, but would fight to prevent the fracturing of the country. The South, meanwhile, had gone too far to listen.

Lincoln's opposite, Confederate President Jefferson Davis, was already occupying his office and planning how best to take over Union garrisons in

Above: The Southern economy was based on agriculture. The major cash crops, cotton and tobacco, were grown most profitably with slave labor.

Below: The election of Abraham Lincoln (1809-65) as President proved to be the catalyst that drove the Southern states to secede.

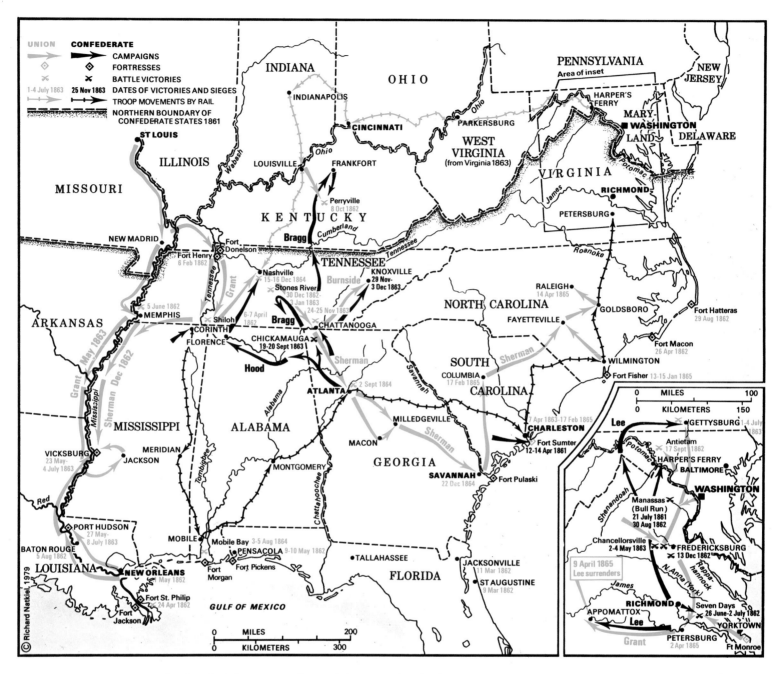

Above: The major
campaigns of the
American Civil War
covered the entire South.
There were also raids into
the Union and battles in
the far West.

Below: Jefferson Davis
(1808-09) was the
Confederate President.

the South. There were three of these in Florida, far
from the centers of government; it was on the fourth
garrison that the attention of the whole country
came to rest – Fort Sumter, in Charleston Harbor.

Jefferson Davis was not new to war. He had been
educated at West Point and had served as Secretary
of War in the Pierce administration. Privately a
genial and sociable man, in public Davis lacked
many of the elements of leadership that Lincoln
possessed in abundance. A subordinate once wrote
of Davis, 'He lacks system, is very slow, does not
discriminate between important and unimportant
matters, has no practical knowledge of the working
of our military system in the field.' Beyond that, in
his public duties Davis was cold, inflexible, and
quarrelsome. He also considered himself a great
military strategist, and throughout the war supervised the entire Confederate war effort – most often
to its detriment. Though he began by appointing to
command a much stronger slate of generals than
Lincoln did, in the long run Davis was to demon–

strate an extraordinary talent for encouraging bad
generals and neglecting good ones.

The importance and the vulnerability of Fort
Sumter had become clear even before Lincoln or
Davis had taken office. After South Carolina
seceded, state authorities sent a commission to
President James Buchanan to arrange for transfer of
Federal property to the Confederacy. Buchanan,
who was not entirely unsympathetic to the South,
met the commissioners unofficially and told them he
would not change the status quo in Charleston
Harbor. But soon after this the status quo did change
ominously. Acting on his own, Major Robert
Anderson, Federal commander in the harbor,
loaded his men on boats and took them from the old
Revolutionary Fort Moultrie, near the mainland, to
the more defensible Fort Sumter, an unfinished
pentagonal brick edifice three miles out in the
harbor. The significance of Anderson's move was
not lost on Confederate authorities. In January
President Buchanan sent a boat of provisions to the

fort, which was low on both food and munitions; the boat was fired on from the South Carolina mainland and turned back. The state government decreed that no supplies of any kind were to be allowed in. By the time Lincoln took office Fort Sumter was isolated and running out of food.

In dealing with the problem Lincoln had several options, none of them encouraging. Secretary of State Seward and aged General-in-Chief Winfield Scott urged that the fort be evacuated. Less sober voices urged offensive action. At length the President decided neither to abandon the fort nor to initiate hostilities, but rather to send a boatload of provisions to the garrison. In notifying the governor of South Carolina of that action Lincoln was in effect challenging the Confederates to respond: if hostilities were to begin, it must be the South's doing. The next day, 7 April, the response came: General Pierre G T Beauregard, Confederate commander in Charleston, cut off communications between Charleston and the fort and began to organize Confederate forces in the harbor. On 11 April Beauregard sent a demand for evacuation to Major Anderson. Sumter's commander, realizing the terrible momentum that was gathering about his command, replied that he would evacuate on 15 April unless he was attacked or received further orders from Washington. Suspecting, correctly, that this would not satisfy the Confederate authorities, Anderson assured the aides who delivered the ultimatum, 'Gentlemen, if you do not batter the fort to pieces about us, we shall be starved out in a few days.'

The momentum of forces rolled on, pulled by the seemingly irresistible magnet of war. At 3:20 in the morning on 12 April the next note came to Major Anderson: 'we have the honor to notify you that

[Beauregard] will open the fire . . . in one hour from this time.' Greatly upset, Major Anderson accompanied the Confederate messengers back to their boat. Pressing their hands in farewell, he choked, 'If we never meet in this world again, God grant that we may meet in the next.' (Among Anderson's acquaintances on the other side was Beauregard, his artillery instructor at West Point.)

Surrounding Fort Sumter in a wide circle on the mainland and islands around the harbor, the guns of the Confederacy were aimed and ready. Learning of Anderson's final words, General Beauregard sent firing orders at about four in the morning to Captain George S James and the James Island battery. Captain James positioned his men. When they were ready he turned to his friend Roger A Pryor and said to him, 'You are the only man to whom I would give

Above: General Winfield Scott, hero of the Mexican War, led the Union armies.

Left: P G T Beauregard, Confederate Commander of Charleston, also led the rebel armies at the First Battle of Manassas in July 1861.

Left: A contemporary map of Charleston Harbor shows the position of Fort Sumter and the attacking batteries.

Below: Major Robert Anderson, USA, commanded the Union garrison at Fort Sumter.

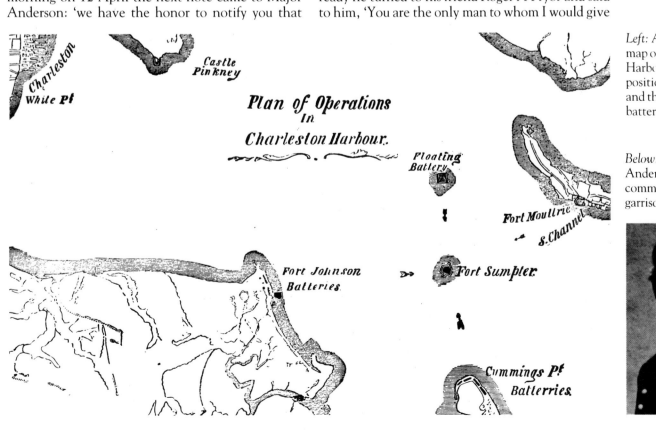

Right: The city of Charleston, South Carolina, suffered some shell damage during the siege of Fort Sumter.

Below: A panoramic photograph of Fort Sumter taken after the Union capitulation.

up the honor of firing the first gun of the war.' Shaken, Pryor declined. At 4:30 in the morning of 12 April 1861, Captain James pulled the firing lanyard of a ten-inch mortar, and the first shot of the war arched into the sky.

As it happened, it was a rather good shot, bursting about a hundred feet over the center of Fort Sumter. The reverberation spread out over the harbor, brought Confederate soldiers to the parapets, raised citizens from their beds in Charleston. It seemed that a thrill of mingled fear and excitement swept through the whole city. Within a few minutes a storm of fire erupted from the 30 guns and 17 mortars of the Confederate batteries around the harbor.

It was not until after daylight that Federal guns began responding from within the fort. The slow rate of return fire showed the Confederates that the Federals were low on ammunition and were mounting only token resistance. Moreover, Northern shells had little effect on the well-protected Southern gun emplacements. Off one of these, a floating ironclad battery, the enemy shot bounced away like peas. The Rebel shot and shell tore holes in the brick masonry of Fort Sumter but did not seriously damage it. After three hours of steady firing there were no casualties to either side. Within the fort the spirits of the defenders were oddly elated. Directing the Federal batteries was Captain Abner Doubleday, later to be known, inaccurately, as the founder of baseball. Doubleday's relief commander

appeared and joked, 'Doubleday, what in the world is the matter here, and what is all this uproar about?' Doubleday responded in kind: 'There is a trifling difference of opinion between us and our neighbors opposite, and we are trying to settle it.'

Three Federal warships appeared outside the harbor in midmorning. The defenders in the fort cheered and flag salutes were exchanged, but after a few hours the ships turned and sailed away. Meanwhile, General Beauregard was trying an experiment. The battery at Fort Moultrie had a furnace to

Above: Fort Sumter was one of four Federal garrisons within the new Confederacy.

Above: Charleston was a major Confederate port for blockade running until its capture in 1865.

Right: Fort Sumter was shelled for almost 34 hours before surrendering.

prepare hot shot – cannonballs heated red-hot before firing. These had started a few small fires within the fort. By the end of the day the fires were out, but Beauregard decided the hot shot was likely to have an effect and determined to make more use of it the next day.

Federal firing ceased at dusk. All through the night the Confederate batteries kept up their pounding while the defenders anxiously tried to sleep. About dawn on 13 April the batteries of Fort Moultrie began pouring hot shot into the fort, and the effects were soon seen: the Union barracks, supposedly fireproof, were in flames. The weak Federal return fire slowed still further, to one shot every five minutes, as soldiers in the fort were detailed to fight the flames and try to keep them from spreading to the magazine. The Confederate cannoneers took to cheering the Federals' efforts to stop the blaze despite the rain of enemy shells. Shortly after noon, the flagstaff of the fort was shot away and quickly repaired. But soon the Stars and Stripes were hauled down and replaced by a white flag.

A detachment was sent by boat to offer aid to the fort. They arrived to find that they had been preceded by ex-Senator Wigfall of Texas, who had apparently rowed out on his own to demand surrender. Wigfall had appeared in front of one of the fort's gun embrasures, to the considerable surprise of the Federal gunners. They had finally pulled Wigfall in before he was killed by his own side's fire. The ensuing negotiations were confused, what with two separate Confederate delegations and Major Anderson's uncertainties and anxieties – he and his men were begrimed with smoke and cinders and near exhaustion. But the outcome was inescapable. The garrison had taken some 4000 shells in 34 hours of nearly continuous bombardment and the Federals had few shells left to fire in reply. Finally Anderson capitulated, saying he would evacuate Fort Sumter on 14 April. Beauregard generously agreed that the Federals could salute their flag with cannons before leaving. By that point there still had been no casualties on either side.

As an ironic fate would have it, men were nonetheless destined to fall as a result of this battle. As the Federals fired their salute to the flag on 14 April, some sparks from the smouldering fire in the fort set

The Confederate flag replaced the Stars and Stripes on the ramparts of Fort Sumter.

Many Charlestonians went out to view the destruction after the fall of Fort Sumter.

off a paper-wrapped cannon cartridge as it was being loaded. The explosion killed Private Daniel Hough and wounded five other soldiers, one of whom soon died. These were the first casualties of the Civil War. After the salute Captain Doubleday formed the men on the parade ground and marched them out to board a Federal steamer, the tattered Stars and Stripes flying, the band playing 'Yankee Doodle,' and Southern soldiers and spectators cheering. Soon the cheering redoubled as Confederate soldiers marched into the fort and the Confederate flag, made of silk by the ladies of Charleston, was run up the flagpole.

That banner would not come down until the very end of the war. Despite massive Federal shelling in the last months, the fort would remain a symbol of Southern defiance from the beginning to the end. There was a long and tragic road to travel between those two points. Few perceived that fact in April of

1861. War seemed rather dashing and decorous at Fort Sumter; to the Southerners it seemed the realization of all their fantasies of how easy it would be to send the Yankees running. All over the South there was rivalry, dancing in the streets, young men joining up in thousands, showing off their grand new uniforms and guns to their families. They dreamed of glory and immortality and the romantic excitement of battle. In Richmond, former President John Tyler cast his lot with the South, and his wife wrote to her mother in New York, 'Subjugate or *bring to terms* such a people! Little do you *dream* at the North of what stuff they are made ... it is a thrilling, melting sight to see the entrances into the city of troops by the trains from all parts of the Southern country, coming as they appear to feel, to the *rescue of old Virginia* ... they joyfully march off to their encampments, apparently congratulating themselves they are so near the scene of action.'

But elsewhere in the South another woman of Virginia, living in sight of Washington, wrote eloquently of her fears and heartbreak:

Everything is broken up. The Seminary is closed; the High School dismissed ... The homes all look desolate ... We are left lonely indeed; our children are all gone – the girls where they may be safer, and the boys, the dear, dear boys, to the camp, to be drilled. Can it be that our country is to be carried on and on to the horrors of civil war? I shut my eyes and hold my breath when the thought of what may come upon us obtrudes itself, and yet I cannot believe it ... I go from room to room, looking first at one thing and then another. The closed piano, the locked bookcase, the nicely arranged tables, the formally placed chairs ... Oh, for someone to put them out of order!

I heard distinctly the drums beating in Washington. As I looked at the Capitol in the distance, I could scarcely believe my senses. That Capitol of which I had always been so proud! Can it be possible that it is no longer *our* capitol? Must this Union, which I was taught to revere, be rent asunder?

John Tyler (1790-1862), 10th President of the United States, was elected to the Confederate Congress.

Left: The Confederates filled the shell holes in the outer walls of the fort with baskets packed with sand, to absorb shot.

CHAPTER II
FIRST AND SECOND MANASSAS

Previous spread: The Second Battle of Manassas, despite the Union retreat, was an incomplete victory.

After the fall of Fort Sumter war fever swept across the country – or rather, the two countries. President Lincoln called for 75,000 three-month volunteers to suppress the Southern rebellion. Four more states seceded – Virginia, Arkansas, Tennessee, and North Carolina. The border states – Delaware, Maryland, Kentucky and Missouri – stayed shakily loyal to the Union, even though the latter three were slave states. Both sides expected a short war, to be won in one or two decisive battles. Certainly no one foresaw the four years of agony that were to come.

There were essentially differences in the strategy and aims of the two sections. The more formidable task was the Union's – in order to conquer the South the North had physically to invade, occupy, and hold its entire territory. This involved unprecedented commitments of men and supplies. On the other hand, the Confederacy's strategy seemed to call for the defensive. As Northern armies advanced into the South their supply lines would steadily become longer and more tenuous as their numbers shrank due to attrition and the necessity of guarding lines of communication. The South thus had the advantage of fighting on and for its own territory,

Below: Southerners flocked to serve 'The Cause' in the early days of the war.

and also had, theoretically at least, the advantage of *interior lines* (because an invading army must stretch around and contain its enemy, that enemy, being more compact, can shift its forces much faster on interior lines of communications).

For these reasons, the South's confidence in its war effort was less fanciful than it might seem. The North was far superior in numbers, arms, industry, roads, ships, and railroads. But it is far harder to conquer than to keep territory; the British learned this in the American Revolution, when their industrial and military superiority were unable to make headway. At the beginning of the war the South probably had at least as good a chance of winning its war as the American colonies had of winning theirs. Moreover, Jefferson Davis confidently expected Great Britain and France to come to the rescue of the Confederacy; the threat of losing Southern cotton, Davis said, would bring them to the Confederate cause: King Cotton would cinch recognition of the Confederacy from across the Atlantic. In this as in many other things, Davis miscalculated seriously. Great Britain at the beginning of the war had enough surplus cotton to last two years, and after that time found other sources.

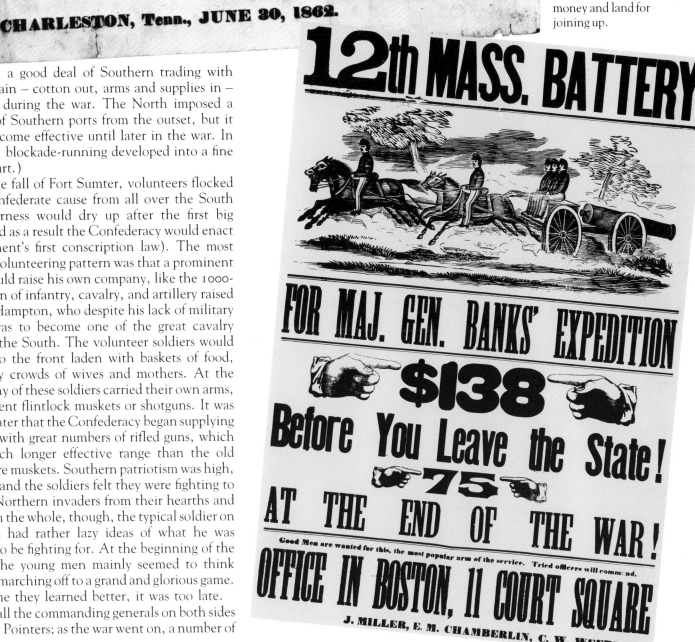

FREEMEN!
AVOID CONSCRIPTION!

The undersigned desires to raise a Company for the Confederate States service, and for that purpose I call upon the people of the Counties of Jefferson and Hawkins, Tenn., to meet promptly at Russellville, on SATURDAY, JULY 19th, 1862, and organize a Company.

By so doing you will avoid being taken as Conscripts, for that Act will now be enforced by order of the War Department. Rally, then, my Countrymen, to your Country's call.

S. M. DENNISON,
Of the Confederate States Army.

CHARLESTON, Tenn., JUNE 30, 1862.

Left: By the second summer of the war, Confederate enlistments had fallen, and conscription laws had been enacted.

Below: The Union Army offered bounties of money and land for joining up.

12th MASS. BATTERY
FOR MAJ. GEN. BANKS' EXPEDITION
☞ $138 ☜
Before You Leave the State!
☞ 75 ☜
AT THE END OF THE WAR !
Good Men are wanted for this, the most popular arm of the service. Tried officers will command.
OFFICE IN BOSTON, 11 COURT SQUARE
J. MILLER, E. M. CHAMBERLIN, C. W. WEEBER.

(However, a good deal of Southern trading with Great Britain – cotton out, arms and supplies in – did go on during the war. The North imposed a blockade of Southern ports from the outset, but it did not become effective until later in the war. In the South, blockade-running developed into a fine maritime art.)

After the fall of Fort Sumter, volunteers flocked to the Confederate cause from all over the South (this eagerness would dry up after the first big battles, and as a result the Confederacy would enact the continent's first conscription law). The most common volunteering pattern was that a prominent citizen would raise his own company, like the 1000-man Legion of infantry, cavalry, and artillery raised by Wade Hampton, who despite his lack of military training was to become one of the great cavalry leaders of the South. The volunteer soldiers would head off to the front laden with baskets of food, cheered by crowds of wives and mothers. At the outset many of these soldiers carried their own arms, often ancient flintlock muskets or shotguns. It was not until later that the Confederacy began supplying its armies with great numbers of rifled guns, which had a much longer effective range than the old smoothbore muskets. Southern patriotism was high, of course, and the soldiers felt they were fighting to keep the Northern invaders from their hearths and homes. On the whole, though, the typical soldier on both sides had rather lazy ideas of what he was supposed to be fighting for. At the beginning of the conflict, the young men mainly seemed to think they were marching off to a grand and glorious game. By the time they learned better, it was too late.

Nearly all the commanding generals on both sides were West Pointers; as the war went on, a number of

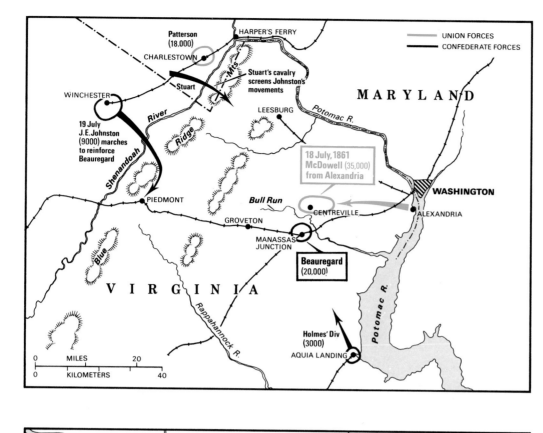

The battlefield at Manassas was less than a day's march from the Federal capital at Washington.

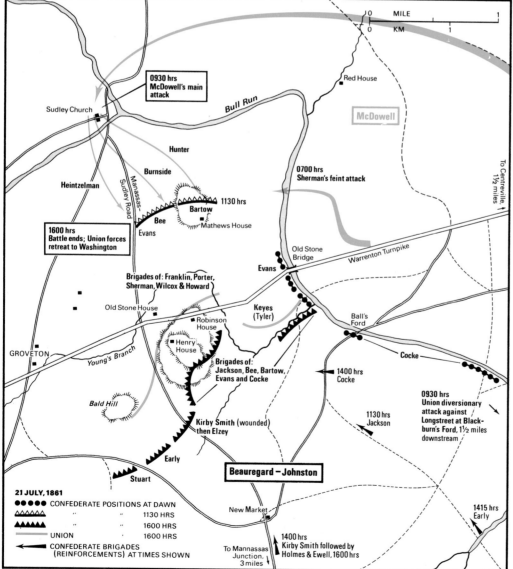

untrained leaders of genius arose, among then Nathan Bedford Forest. But since military tradition was stronger in the South, the Confederacy got more than its share of the best military minds of the time; at the beginning of the war the North had no one to compare to Robert E Lee, the two Johnstons, and Beauregard. This superiority of Confederate generalship in the early part of the war was clear to all concerned in the two great battles fought on a little stream called the Bull Run, near Manassas, Virginia.

Having resigned his commission in the US Army – and in the process of declining an offer to command all Union forces – Robert Edward Lee was made a general in the Confederate army and given overall command of operations in his beloved home

Below: The elaborate uniforms worn by both sides early in the war confused troops who found it difficult to distinguish friend and foe.

General James Longstreet CSA (1821-1904).

The American Civil War saw the first use of trains as troop transports.

soon to achieve statehood). Lee sent 11,000 men under General Joseph E Johnston to Harpers Ferry, near the entrance to Virginia's Shenandoah Valley, and 22,000 under General Pierre G T Beauregard to Manassas Junction, some 25 miles southwest of Washington. Lincoln, despite objections that Union forces were too green, ordered General Irvin McDowell to drive Beauregard away from the important Manassas rail junction. Most of McDowell's 30,600 men were three-month volunteers and militia; only 800 were regular army. In support of McDowell, General Robert Patterson was ordered to keep Johnston in the Shenandoah in order to prevent his reinforcing Beauregard.

On 16 July, McDowell began advancing from Washington toward what everyone seemed to know would be the first great convulsion of the war. Many felt it would be the last. Confidently, the Union soldiers shouted, 'On to Richmond!' Accompanying the Federal army were swarms of reporters, Congressmen, ladies with parasols and picnic baskets and assorted sightseers – all off to see the war as if it were a fireworks show.

Marching on the Warrenton Turnpike, McDowell's Federal army reached Centreville, near Manassas, Virginia, on 18 July. At that point Beauregard's forces were vulnerable, though McDowell had no idea of that fact. Since the Union forces had become highly disorganized during the march, McDowell did not try a fullscale offensive (if he had, it might well has been successful). Meanwhile, Beauregard had received thorough intelligence concerning Union dispositions from a network of spies in Washington. He asked General Johnston to bring his forces over from the Shenandoah, where Patterson proved unable to contest their departure. On the 18th McDowell did try a reconnaissance in force against Beauregard's right. After a brisk skirmish at Blackburn's Ford on the Bull Run, the Federals were sent running back by the Confederates. The Southern commander in that skirmish was General James Longstreet, soon to be one of the great corps leaders of Robert E Lee's army. (In the South the affair at Blackburn's Ford is called the First Battle of Bull Run; to add to the confusion, the Northern names for the two large battles around the stream are the First and Second Bull Run).

McDowell's hesitation on the 28th allowed time for Johnston to move his 12,000 men east from the Shenandoah Valley. Most of that journey was made by railroad – the first major strategic troop movement by railroad in history. Among Johnston's generals was a strange, laconic brigade commander named Thomas J Jackson.

McDowell and Beauregard had been classmates at West Point and had studied the same tactics. Perhaps for that reason, they made identical plans for an offensive on 19 July: feint with the left, attack with the right. If both had been successful, the results could have been comic indeed – after brushing past each other like a swinging door, the Confederates might have continued right into

state of Virginia. In June and July of 1861 Americans began killing one another: Union forces were defeated near Fort Monroe, Virginia, and Federal general George B McClellan secured the western counties of Virginia for the Union (this area was

Washington and the Federals march into Richmond. But on the morning of the 19th, McDowell got his offensive underway first, and thereafter Beauregard and Johnston were on the defensive. McDowell made his feint on the Southern right, mounted a secondary attack on the enemy center, and took his right wing on a wide envelopment, marching the troops 15 miles through the broken and difficult landscape to attack the Rebel left flank. (Flank attacks have been feared since time immemorial, since return fire cannot be directed down the line. An army can only receive a flank attack by turning its flank to meet it, which takes time and skill to accomplish under fire. Otherwise the victims' line is rolled up like a rug.)

Union general McDowell's plan was a perfectly good one, but it ran afoul of several problems. First, his troops were too inexperienced to execute with dispatch the intended wide envelopment of the Southern left flank. Second, Confederate observers on Signal Hill saw the movement and sent word to Beauregard: 'look out for your left; you are turned.' Third, Beauregard had seen a cloud of dust on his left and realized the attack along the Warrenton Turnpike was a bluff to cover the move on his left.

He began shifting divisions over to his left to oppose the oncoming Federals in the vicinity of Henry House Hill. As the Federals marched they could hear the whistles of the trains bringing Johnston's men to the battlefront. These arrivals were formed up on the railroad platform and marched directly into line. (Though Johnston was the ranking commander, by mutual consent Beauregard supervised the operations because he knew the ground better. However, there was a bitter postwar wrangle between the two men about who was really responsible for the victory.)

Confident that every one of them could whip seven Yankees, the Confederate troops advanced from Henry House Hill toward the enemy. But then the Federals smashed into the Rebels, driving them back onto the hill. For nearly everyone on the field it was the first experience of firing on foes who a short time before had been fellow countrymen; there is no report that this fact slowed the pace of battle. It seemed that the Federals were going to sweep the Rebels back down Henry House Hill. But defending that position was Thomas J Jackson and the brigade he had trained. He formed his men into a defensive nucleus on the hilltop. Seeing that stand, Con-

The Union troops, though brave, were inexperienced and badly led.

federate general Bernard E Bee entered history in his last moments of life: 'Look at Jackson's Brigade,' Bee shouted to his men'; 'It stands like a stone wall! Rally behind the Virginians!' And rally they did, stopping the advancing Federal army in their tracks. And forever after, the general who led that stand would be called Stonewall Jackson, his men the Stonewall Brigade.

As Beauregard continued to strip his right and send men to the left, the Confederate line firmed up around Jackson on Henry House Hill. Finally Jackson led a counterattack on the Union right flank; sweeping around the hill in support rode the Rebel cavalrymen of young J E B ('Jeb') Stuart, another leader of that day destined for greatness. Jeb's men tore into a battalion of red-pantalooned New York Zouaves, inflicting heavy casualties. At the most critical moment, just after two o'clock in the afternoon, on the Southern left, a Union artillery officer held his fire, mistaking blue-clad Rebel troops in his front for Federals; as a result, two powerful batteries fell into Southern hands and the Federals began to retreat. Now was Beauregard's great chance to pursue the enemy and annihilate them. However, at just that moment, Beauregard echoed the mistake of the Federal artillery com-

Below: The New York 69th, an Irish regiment, was commanded by Colonel Michael Corcoran.

mander: receiving a report that a large Federal force was moving on his supplies near Manassas, Beauregard pulled troops from his attacking force to meet this threat. But the threat was a false alarm – it was Confederates marching towards the supplies, not Yankees. As Beauregard's advance slowed, dusk came on. The Confederacy had won the field that day of the first Manassas, but it was too late to pursue the enemy.

The Federals commenced an orderly retreat from the battlefield, moving up the Warrenton Turnpike. The Federal column, including numbers of civilian spectators who had not found the battle to be as

much fun as they had expected, had to constrict to pass over a stone bridge over the Bull Run. Suddenly a Rebel battery dropped a few shells into the dense column near the bridge. There was an instant panic that quickly snowballed into utter chaos:

Above: The New York Zouaves were attacked by Jeb Stuart's 1st Virginia Cavalry.

For three miles, hosts of Federal troops – all detached from their regiments, all mingled in one disorderly rout – were fleeing along the road, but mostly through the lots on either side. Army wagons, sutlers' teams, and private carriages, choked the passage, tumbling against each other, amid clouds of dust, and sickening sights and sounds. Hacks, containing unlucky spectators of the late afray, were smashed like glass, and the occupants were lost sight of in the debris. Horses, flying wildly from the battlefield, many of them in death agony, galloped at random forward, joining in the stampede. Those on foot who could catch them rode them bareback ... Wounded men, lying along the banks ... appealed with raised hands to those who rode horses, begging to be lifted behind ... Then the artillery, such as was saved, came thundering along, smashing and overpowering everything. The regular cavalry, I record it to their shame, joined in the melee, adding to its terrors, for they rode down footmen without mercy ... Who ever saw such a flight? ... It did not slack in the least until Centreville was reached.

On 22 July Washington was inundated by the broken remains of its great army, which had become a mob of jaded, dirty, and demoralized men. Of that terrible day, poet Walt Whitman was later to remember,

But the hour, the day, the night pass'd, and whatever returns, an hour, a day, a night like that can never again return. The President, recovering himself, begins that very night ... reorganizing his forces, and placing himself in positions for future and surer work. If there were nothing else of Abraham Lincoln for history to stamp him

Below: A Confederate Zouave Regiment known as the Louisiana Tigers fought at 1st Manassas.

with, it is enough . . . that he endured that hour, that day, bitterer than gall – indeed a crucifixion day . . . and resolv'd to lift himself and the Union out of it.

On the Confederate side there was a great and understandable jubilation over the triumph at Manassas. But the victory led to a dangerous overconfidence. Rebel soldiers had been confirmed in their illusion of invincibility. Jefferson Davis assured friends that European recognition of the Confederacy was now certain, that the war was virtually over except for the mopping up. Security was relaxed; enlistments fell; politicians in Richmond began scheming to succeed Davis in six years. Thus it is not surprising that before the war was over a Richmond editor was to write, 'All in all, the victory of Manassas proved the greatest misfortune that could have befallen the Confederacy.'

Perhaps the South should have studied the casualty figures; they would have found the Union army had not been seriously damaged. Indeed, by the later standards of the war the First Manassas was not a particularly bloody contest – the South had 387 killed, 1582 wounded, 12 missing, for a total of 1981 casualties of the 32,232 engaged; the Union suffered 418 killed, 1011 wounded, 1216 missing, for a total of 2645 casualties of 28,452 engaged. The contrast in the numbers of missing is notable; but the fact remained that the Union army was only marginally

more hurt than the Confederate – and the North had virtually endless supplies of manpower, whereas the South was severely limited in that regard. The day after the First Manassas, a young Federal general named George B McClellan took command in Washington and from the shattered Union forces of the First Manassas began rebuilding the army.

Stonewall Jackson went on to his Shenandoah Valley Campaign of summer 1862. During that operation, Jackson kept three Federal armies tied up in the Valley and thereby helped to stymie Union General McClellan's Peninsular Campaign on Richmond with his new Army of the Potomac. During the Seven Days Battles that surged around Richmond during McClellan's campaign, Confederate General J E Johnston, one of the heroes of the First Manassas, was severely wounded. Johnston was replaced by General Robert E Lee; it was Lee who finished the job of driving the Army of the Potomac away from Richmond and, before long, out of Virginia entirely.

After tying up the enemy armies in the Shenandoah and keeping them from reinforcing McClellan, Stonewall Jackson hurried east to join Lee in the Seven Days Battles. As soon as Jackson's forces left the Shenandoah, new orders went out from Washington: the three Federal armies that had futilely chased Jackson were to be consolidated into one army under General John Pope, who was then to march South from Washington and draw the Confederate army away from Richmond. But the plan was soon changed in light of Union failures in the Seven Days, and a new plan developed – McClellan was to move his forces around by water to unite with Pope; with the resulting army of 130,000 men, the Federals would descend into Virginia to annihilate Lee's army of 50,000. Federal intelligence estimates had more than doubled Lee's actual numbers; in contrast, Lee had a perfectly clear idea of the daunting prospect he was up against. It was the first great challenge of his career.

The new commander of the Confederate Army of Northern Virginia was an unusual man for a soldier. So soft-spoken, courtly, and religious was Lee that many of his soldiers dubbed him 'Granny.' It was not long before they saw him more accurately: this mild-mannered Virginian aristocrat was one of the most aggressive and brilliant fighting generals who ever lived. His father was Revolutionary War hero 'Light-Horse Harry' Lee. At West Point Robert had been second in his class and the only cadet in history never to receive a demerit. As a young officer in the Mexican War he quickly gained a reputation as the most promising – and handsomest – soldier in the army. Very simply, he was from the beginning one of those people around whom an aura of greatness seems to gather. His place in history, which is assured and immortal, in the end would have as much to do with his remarkable character as with his innovative boldness on the battlefield. But it is a

Left: Throughout the war the Confederate Army lacked enough uniforms. The standard gray issue was rarely seen.

strange position he occupies: later called by Winston Churchill 'the greatest of Americans,' Lee was a primary leader of a rebellion that aimed to destroy the United States. He came to that position circuitously. He believed neither in slavery nor in secession, and was certainly patriotic enough before the war. The agonizing decision he made at the beginning of the conflict is indicative of pre-war attitudes and loyalties: like many Americans of that era, Lee placed loyalty to his home state above loyalty to the United States. In his resignation from the US Army, Lee said he could not raise his hand against Virginians; if they seceded, so must he.

It was not long before Lee was virtually deified by his Army of Northern Virginia. It can be said that he was held in similar respect by his enemies – everyone knew he could be counted on to be the most dangerous man on the field. Moreover, the Army of Northern Virginia had an outstanding staff of subordinates. The great Stonewall Jackson was known as Lee's right arm. In addition there were the over-cautious but hard fighting James Longstreet, the impetuous A P Hill, choleric Daniel H Hill, and 25-year-old Jeb Stuart, one of the greatest cavalrymen of all time, who fulfilled his function of being the eyes of Lee's army with extraordinary effectiveness and dash.

Such generals combined with a fighting body of the highest spirit made for one of the great armies of history, one already legendary during its own brief existence. But it is also true that there were deep and abiding weaknesses in both the command structure and army, and these weaknesses eventually added up to defeat. Chief among these weaknesses was that both Lee and the Confederate government paid too little attention to logistics, especially the need to feed and clothe the army properly. For much of the war Southern soldiers marched and fought hungry, ragged, and often soleless, even when the Confederacy had abundant supplies. The availability of arms and powder was remarkably dependable

Far left: The Confederate Cavalry were usually mounted on their own horses. Until the Union victory at Brandy Station in 1863, they were considered invincible.

Below: Albert Sidney Johnston CSA (1803-62) was one of the many promising generals who joined the rebel army.

throughout the war, but soldiers need more than weapons in order to fight. Beyond that, Lee often gave vague orders, leaving much leeway for his generals; with a subordinate of genius like Stonewall Jackson, the results could be spectacular, but with lesser generals there were often misunderstandings. And Lee arguably gave too much of his attention to his beloved home state of Virginia, leaving large-scale strategy to the unreliable attentions of Jefferson Davis (though this was more the fault of Davis than of Lee). Other systematic weaknesses in the Army of Northern Virginia emerged during various campaigns, but there was a final problem with the whole army worth mentioning: the pernicious effects of success itself. As the list of miraculous victories grew longer and longer, first his army and then Robert E Lee himself fell prey to the dangerous myth that they were invincible.

But all these things were unknown in July of 1862. By then Lee had driven McClellan from the gates of Richmond, but he faced the prospect of a grand combination of McClellan and Pope's forces that would, if successfully accomplished, spell almost certain doom for the Confederacy. On 14 July Pope began moving his forces south in Virginia, intending to take over the railroad junction at Gordonsville and then attack Lee, who for the moment was still protecting the Confederate capitol from further efforts by McClellan. An observer watched Lee as he grappled with this daunting situation:

When contemplating any great undertaking or a vast strategic combination, General Lee had an abstracted manner that was altogether unlike his usual one. He would seek some level sward and

pace mechanically up and down with the regularity of a sentinel on his beat; his head would be bent as if in deep meditation, while his left hand unconciously stroked his thick iron-grey beard.

Soon Stonewall Jackson was summoned; Lee now knew what he was going to do. Jackson and A P Hill were ordered north with 24,000 men to confront Pope, to draw him away from the safety of Washington. Above all Pope had to be dealt with before McClellan could reinforce him; time was running short if that was to be done. As always, Lee had examined his opponent carefully and knew his man. In this case, he knew he was dealing not with a worthy opponent but with a blustering fool. This may be seen in Pope's first address to his new command, in which he crowed, 'Let us understand each other. I come to you from the West, where we

Far left: Confederate fortifications at Manassas made use of the supplies shipped by barrel to that railroad junction.

Below: One of the Union brigades at Manassas was commanded by General Ambrose Burnside.

The Confederacy practiced a 'scorched earth' policy before the advancing Union armies.

have always seen the backs of our enemies.' Lee took an uncharacteristically angry attitude toward this particular opponent; the 'miscreant' Pope, Lee said, must be 'suppressed.'

Jackson set off with his and Hill's divisions to execute Lee's orders. He first planned to smash Pope's vanguard at Culpeper, Virginia, then to defeat the rest in detail, one corps at a time. But due to unwonted slowness, Jackson fumbled his initial strategy. On 9 August the advancing Confederates found themselves opposed by General Nathaniel Banks at Cedar Mountain. The Federals came on strongly and pushed Jackson's men back, but a crashing counterattack by A P Hill ended the enemy advance. During that encounter one of Jackson's officers watched his commander in action:

Jackson came dashing across the road in great excitement. He drew his sword, took the battle-flag from my man, waved it over his head, and cried: 'Where is my Stonewall Brigade? Forward men, Forward!' Our men followed and drove everything before them. Jackson usually is an indifferent and slouchy looking man, but his whole person changed; his face was lit with the inspiration of heroism. Even the old sorrel horse seemed endowed with the form of an Arabian.

Pope's advance had been slowed, but no more. And now McClellan began pulling his Army of the Potomac away from Richmond by water and moving to combine with Pope. The immediate threat to the capitol over, Lee moved with Longstreet's division to join Jackson and march to the east of Pope's army, trying to maneuver to a position between him and both Washington and McClellan. This plan miscarried; because of poor staff work and a surprise attack on Jeb Stuart's camp (18 August) that captured Lee's plans, the Confederates were unable to march east of Pope. Finally both armies came to rest facing one another across the Rappahannock River, both making probing attacks with their cavalry. The report came to Lee that McClellan was now five days away from juncture with Pope. In effect, the Confederates were racing with McClellan to get to Pope first. At that critical juncture in the history of the Confederacy, the combination of Lee and Jackson first revealed the genius for which history remembers them.

For the first, but not the last, time, Lee contradicted an ancient and virtually ironbound rule of military strategy: Do not divide forces in the face of the enemy. In this case, it was an enemy that outnumbered Lee 75,000 to 55,000. The extraordinary bold plan was this: holding Pope in place on the Rappahannock with Longstreet's thinly-

Many sailors in the Confederate Navy served in Artillery batteries

Right: George B McClellan (1826-85) became Commander in Chief of the Union Army in December 1861.

spaced forces, Lee sent Jackson and Jeb Stuart on a wide envelopment, first northwest, then east, around Pope's army. Jackson's command left on 25 August; his footsoldiers duplicated the feats of marching they had demonstrated in the Valley Campaign, when they earned the title 'foot cavalry.' On the first day they marched 26 miles, the second day 36 miles. A participant remembered the utter secretiveness that Jackson maintained during the maneuver:

No man save one in that corps, whatever may have been his rank, knew our destination. The man said of Jackson that his piety expressed itself in obeying the injunction, 'Let not thy left hand know what thy right hand doeth.' No intelligence of intended Confederate movements ever reached the enemy by any slip of his. The orders to his division chiefs were like this: 'March to a cross-road; a staff-officer there will inform you which fork to take; and so to the next fork, where you will find a courier with a sealed direction pointing out the road.'

This extreme reticence was very uncomfortable and annoying to his subordinate commanders, and was sometimes carried too far; but it was the real secret of the reputation for ubiquity which he acquired, and which was so well expressed by General McClellan in one of his dispatches: 'I am afraid of Jackson; he will turn up where least expected.'

At least McClellan had the sense to expect the unexpected from Stonewall Jackson. In the ensuing days that led up to the convulsion of the Battle of Second Manassas, General Pope resolutely refused to believe that Jackson was behaving in anything but a timid and predictable fashion.

Pope's first surprise came on the evening of 27 August, when Jackson's men swamped the Union supply dump at Manassas. There the hungry Confederates eagerly fell to destroying what they could not carry; but first they had themselves the feast of a lifetime:

The quantity of booty was very great, and the amount of luxuries absolutely incredible. It was exceedingly amusing to see here a ragged fellow regaling himself with a box of pickled oysters or potted lobster; there another cutting into a cheese of enormous size, or emptying a bottle of champagne; while hundreds were engaged in opening the packages of boots and shoes and other clothing, and fitting themselves with articles of apparel to replace their own tattered garments.

After torching the remaining supplies, Jackson and Stuart pulled their forces away and, as far as Federal intelligence was concerned, vanished into thin air. General Pope, finding Jackson unexpectedly on his rear and the Federal supply line at Manassas destroyed, pulled his army away to the north on 26 August. This was what Lee had been waiting for; he took Longstreet's corps away from the Rappahannock, marching to meet Jackson. Meanwhile, Pope's blustering confusions continued; insisting that Jackson was retreating toward the Shenandoah Valley, Pope vowed to find and destroy him. Finally the Union army of 75,000 men was concentrated squarely between Jackson's force of 24,000 and Longstreet's still-distant 30,000. Here was a golden opportunity for the North: crush Jackson and then turn on Longstreet. The trouble was, Pope could not find Jackson, despite frantic efforts to do so. Too, from start to very near finish Pope ignored Longstreet entirely. Stonewall Jackson once summarized the essence of his strategy as, 'Always mystify, mislead, and surprise the enemy if possible.' He had achieved both those aims, in spades, with General John Pope.

Nonetheless, with a large enemy army between

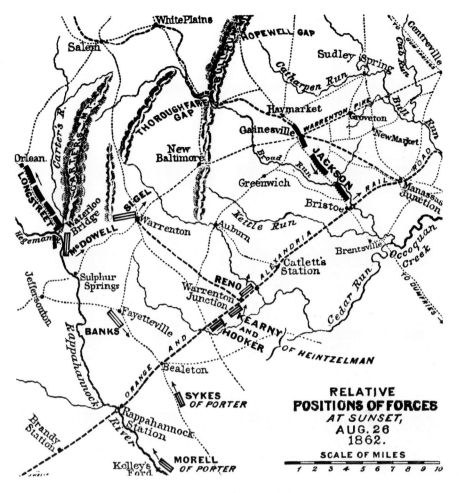

RELATIVE POSITIONS OF FORCES AT SUNSET, AUG. 26 1862.

SCALE OF MILES
1 2 3 4 5 6 7 8 9 10

their divided forces the Confederates were in a desperate situation, one that might well have proved fatal if their opponent had possessed a modicum of sense. Jackson's problem was: how to hold Pope at bay until Longstreet arrived, how to attack if possible and still leave room to retreat. About 27 August Jackson found the place to do all those things – an unfinished railroad cut at the foot of Stony Ridge. It was an ideal defensive position, attackers having to make their way across a deep excavation. Behind the cut were mountain passes serviceable for retreat. On 27-28 August Jackson moved his forces to that position circuitously, in three detachments, and then literally hid his army in the woods behind the railroad cut. Meanwhile the confusion of the Union command mounted, Pope sending his forces marching up and down the area in a futile effort to locate Jackson.

On 28 August the Federals were in Groveton, unaware of Jackson's presence nearby. At that point Jackson made a historic gamble, a bigger one still than Lee had been made in dividing his army. With less than a third of the forces of the enemy, Jackson moved out and attacked the Federals, thereby revealing his position. It was a decision so bold as to seem foolhardy. The reason for it was that Jackson wanted to make sure Pope stayed away from strong defenses at nearby Centreville; if they pulled back to that position, the Federals could wait for the oncoming McClellan with impunity.

So Jackson moved out and struck the Federals near Groveton. A fierce skirmish developed as Pope

Above: The area around Manassas was crossed by creeks and rivers.

Below: General Edmund Kirby Smith CSA (1824-93).

Above: Confederate troops commanded by Stonewall Jackson pillaged the Union supplies at Manassas Junction.

Opposite: General John Pope commanded the Union forces at the Second Battle of Manassas.

turned his army to smash the supposedly retreating Jackson, meanwhile sending telegrams to Washington proclaiming victory over Jackson and saying Lee was in precipitous retreat to Richmond. Some of his officers tried to warn him of Longstreet's approach; Pope refused to listen. Now the Confederates were ready to engage the enemy before McClellan could arrive. The stage was set for the Battle of Second Manassas.

On the morning of 29 August 1862, General Pope threw 62,000 men against 20,000 Confederates, most of whom were again entrenched behind the railroad cut. The tactics of the Federal attack were classically stupid: a frontal assault on a strong position, executed in a piecemeal and uncoordinated fashion. In the ensuing course of the war a simple formula would be revealed: One man behind cover was worth three men charging at him. It is because of battles like Second Manassas that this formula evolved; but there was much blood to be shed before this idea filtered into the brains of commanding officers.

A Southern soldier recalled the Federal attacks on the 29th:

It was startling to hear the simultaneous crash of a dozen batteries on our left. This was an effort of General Pope to demoralize Jackson's troops preparatory to charging . . . [The railroad] cut was not more than half a mile long . . . The Federals moved forward . . . in plain view. Advancing to within a hundred yards of the cut, they halted a second and then sprang forward with a long-drawn 'huzzah' ringing from their 10,000 throats. On they went until half the distance to the cut and then the smoke, flash and roar of 4000 well-aimed guns burst from the Confederate entrenchment, and a wild, reckless and terrifying Southern yell echoed and re-echoed through the woodlands. And scarcely had it ceased to reverberate when the smoke lifted and disclosed the survivors fleeing for dear life . . . Three such assaults were made on the railroad before the Yanks, on that part of their line, decided they had had enough.

All morning long the Union attacks continued; all were driven back with heavy losses. But the Confederates were increasingly desperate as the morning wore on. Another Confederate soldier remembered:

Just as his dispositions . . . were complete, Jackson heard from Longstreet, who promised him aid in two hours. The shock could be delayed, however, only a few minutes, and Jackson, feeling the imminence of the crisis, started down his line to communicate to his troops, worn with fatigue and suspense, his own heaven-born faith and Longstreet's assurance of help. I rode along the line with him, and all he said was: 'Two hours, men, only two hours; in two hours you will have help. You must stand it two hours.'

It was the crisis of the campaign . . . The enemy came right on until within two hundred yards and then broke into the rush of the charge. The officer commanding the leading center brigade, who was riding a powerful coal-black charger, carried the colors in his hand . . . The whole line rushed upon Jackson's men with the enthusiasm of assured victory.

A hundred yards nearer, and the full fire from Jackson's line burst upon them, but . . . it looked as if the gallant fellow on the black horse would be the only man to fall. On the contrary, while many fell and the line wavered, he was miraculously unhurt, and his men rallied and pressed on after him. For a moment it looked as if he would actually leap into the cut upon his foes; the next moment the great horse reared wildly and fell backward, but his heroic rider jammed the color staff into the earth as he went down, only ten yards from the muzzles of Jackson's muskets. The spell that held them together was broken, the advancing line halted and wavered throughout their length – a moment more and the whole magnificent array had melted into a mass of fugitives.

Again Jackson rode down his lines: 'Half an hour men, only half an hour; can you stand it half an hour?'

As ammunition ran out, the Confederate defenders began hurling rocks at the attackers. General Maxcy Gregg walked up and down behind his troops, a sword of Revolutionary vintage in his hand, shouting 'Let us die here, my men, let us die here!' Then, at about 11 in the morning, Longstreet's corp arrived on the Confederate right. In

fact, Longstreet was squarely athwart a large gap in the Federal line; he could have fallen on the Union flank with devastating effect. But as was to be the case so often in the future, Longstreet was over-cautious, worried about the Union corps on his right. Rather than mounting a fullscale attack, then, Longstreet moved some men over to make a demonstration on the Federal center. This sufficed to relieve the pressure on Jackson and to ensure the failure of Pope's offensive.

At the end of the day on 29 August Jackson pulled back from some of his advanced positions. Obtuse as ever, Pope declared that Jackson was retreating (the Federal commander was still oblivious to the presence of Longstreet). Pope ordered his men to pursue the enemy the next day. Lee encouraged

The Second Battle of Manassas marked the first victory in the partnership of Robert E Lee and Stonewall Jackson.

Pope's illusions by letting some carefully-misin-formed Federal prisoners escape back to their own lines; these returned prisoners assured Pope that the enemy was indeed retreating.

Next day, 30 August, the Federals renewed their assault on the Southern lines, which now contained the entire Army of Northern Virginia. Lee let Pope hit Jackson's left, then sent Longstreet against the opposite Union flank. Longsteet remembered that morning:

. . . a heavy fire of shot and shell was being poured into the thick column of the enemy, and in ten minutes their stubborn masses began to waver and give back. For a moment there was chaos; then order returned and they re-formed, apparently to renew the attack. Meanwhile my other eight

pieces reported to me, and from the crest of the little hill the fire of twelve guns cut them down. As the cannon thundered the ranks broke, only to be formed again with dogged determination. A third time the batteries tore the Federals to pieces, and as they fell back under this terrible fire, I sprung everything to the charge. My troops leaped forward with exultant yells, and all along the line we pushed forward.

Now the Federal army was pincered between Longstreet and Jackson. Lee proceeded to swing his forces shut around the enemy like a gate. One of Longstreet's soldiers later painted a vivid picture of that thrilling advance, which was not accomplished without spirited Federal resistance:

We were now loading and firing at the swiftly approaching enemy, who were . . . advancing straight towards us and shouting with their steady hurrah, so different from the Rebel yell. It was a trying moment and proved the metal of the individual man. Some ran, or white with fear cowered behind the Chinn House . . . others yet stood in an irregular form and loaded and fired, ummindful of the dust and noise of the hurtling shell and screaming shot . . .

On came the Yankees in splendid style . . . their line capitally dressed. It was a perfect advance, and some of us forgot to fire our muskets while watching them . . . It was high time to be leaving, we thought, and now our men were turning to fire one good shot before heeling it to the rear, when right behind us there came with a rush and a vim a fresh Rebel brigade aiming straight for the Yankees. They ran over us and we

joined their lines . . . Every man with his head bent sideways and down, like people breasting a hailstorm, for soldiers always charge so, and the Gray and the Blue met with a mighty shock. A tremendous sheet of flame burst from our line; the weaker side went to the ground in a flash, and with a wild yell the Gray swept on toward the six-gun battery that had been sending forth a stream of death for the past hour . . .

When about a hundred yards from them the dense veil [of smoke] lifted . . . and discovered to us that the battery had ceased firing. We could see the muzzles of the guns, their sullen black mouths pointing to us, and behind them the gunners . . . It was for a second only, like the rising of the curtain for a moment on a hideous tableau, only to be dropped as the eye took in the scene in all its horrors . . .

At once came a noise like thunder shock, that

A strong Federal defense allowed the Union Army to retreat in an orderly manner.

seemed as if an earthquake had riven the place. The ground trembled with the concussion. The appalling sound was heard of iron grapeshot tearing its way through space and through bodies of bone, flesh and blood . . . for a second the line was stupefied and nearly senseless from the blow. The ground was covered with victims and the screams of the wounded rose high above the din and were awful to hear.

'Forward, boys! Don't stop now! Forward, Texans!' and with a cry from every throat the Southerners kept on, officers and men together without form or order . . . Up! Still up! until we reached the crest! As the Yankees pulled the lanyards of the loaded pieces our men were among them . . . A terrific shock. A lane of dead in front. Those standing before the muzzles were blown to pieces. . . . There was a frenzied struggle in the semi-darkness around the guns, so violent and tempestuous, so mad and brain-reeling that to recall it is like fixing the memory of a horrible, blood-curdling dream. Every one was wild with uncontrollable delirium.

Then the mists dissolved and the panting, gasping soldiers could see the picture as it was. The battery had been captured by the Texans and every man at the pieces taken prisoner.

Pope and his army were routed, but a stout Federal defense at Henry House Hill saved the army and made an orderly retreat possible. Lee and Jackson had created the first great victory of their immortal partnership.

There was much more to their success than a battle won, however, The Seven Days Battles, Jackson's Shenandoah Valley Campaign and the Second Manassas had really been one gigantic and ultimately victorious campaign of three months' duration. In that time Lee had sent two enormous Federal armies running back to Washington and virtually cleared Virginia of enemy forces. When Lee took command the North had been at the gates of Richmond. Now Lee was only 25 miles from Washington.

In the end, though, the Second Manassas proved to be an incomplete victory. After driving the North from the field Lee tried to maintain the offensive, sending the corps of Jackson and Longstreet around the Federal west flank at Centreville. In this effort the exhausted Rebels discovered their enemy was still ready to fight. Jackson struck the Federals but they resisted strongly even after two corps commanders were killed. In the end the Federals got away to Washington. On the next day Pope's forces were merged into McClellan's command, and that general once again took over operations in the East. Pope was never to command in the field again.

The Second Manassas was the first really devastating engagement of the Civil War. Now the soldiers and civilians of the contending nations were to learn the real costs of war. Confederate casualties were 1481 killed, 7627 wounded, 89 missing, a total of 9197 out of 48,527 engaged – 19 percent casualties. Federal losses were 1724 killed, 8372 wounded, 5958 missing, a total of 16,054 of the 75,696 engaged – 21 percent casualties.

Now Lee had to do something. He could not stay put; his army was in an exposed position near the enemy capitol, where there were enormous masses of soldiers who would sooner or later be coming at him again. Lee knew he did not have sufficient strength to mount a siege of Washington. But it was not in his nature to pull back to safety near Richmond. Lee was above all an aggressive general; thus he decided to keep going, to invade Maryland. In this decision he underestimated his enemy and overestimated his own men. It was Pope, not the Federal soldiers, who had lost the Second Manassas; in battle the Northern men had fought with the same valor as their enemy. But in the aftermath of a great victory great mistakes can be made, even by great leaders.

Above: Major General Wade Hampton CSA (1818-1902).

CHAPTER III

JACKSON'S
SHENANDOAH VALLEY
CAMPAIGN

Previous spread: Jackson's strategy in the Valley necessitated keeping three Union armies separate.

Opposite: Thomas Jonathan Jackson (1824-63) attended West Point and taught at the Virginia Military Institute.

Stonewall Jackson showed his mettle in the Battle of Second Manassas. It was one of his greatest moments, but it was only the climax of a campaign in the Shenandoah Valley of Virginia that has forever stamped Jackson's genius in the annals of military history.

Thomas Jonathan Jackson had not seemed so promising at the outset of his military career. He arrived at West Point an awkward, taciturn mountain boy clad in rough homespun. With great effort he managed to rise from the bottom to nearly the top of his class during his four years. When the Civil War began he was professor of mathematics and natural philosophy at the Virginia Military Institute and already viewed as a strange character. He was a fanatical, brooding and humorless Presbyterian, who never smoked or drank or played cards. He was obsessed with his health and eccentric remedies: during the war he sucked lemons constantly, shunned pepper claiming it made his left leg weak, and kept his right arm raised a good deal of the time saying it improved the circulation.

So peculiar was Jackson that some of his own subordinates questioned his sanity. His obsessive secrecy drove his men close to madness themselves; not only did the enemy never know where Jackson was going, neither did any of his command, much of the time. But it was not long before everyone on both sides understood the military genius of Stonewall Jackson, and thereafter his men were happy to accept any odd notion he devised.

One of his subordinates described Jackson in the field:

Below: Jackson began the war training infantry at Harpers Ferry.

He was mounted on a very ordinary sorrel horse, whose appearance indicated rather short rations. His uniform was well-worn, faded, and covered with ... dust. His cap, originally blue, but now faded and dusty, was ... falling forward upon the visor which nearly touched the point of his nose ... An ordinary saber with an iron scabbard completed his equipment. He was not a graceful rider, and sat his horse carelessly. He looked neither to the right nor to the left, but straight forward, as if that was the one direction in which he cared to think or move. The square and massive lower jaw, covered with a short, thick beard, the firm, set lips, and the preoccupied expression of his whole face were forcibly suggestive of his *nom de guerre,* 'Stonewall,' in their firmness as well as inscrutability.

But this plain, silent soldier, as he appeared on the march, was not always the same. At the first sounds of approaching battle, his whole appearance changed; his movements became quick and energetic; his eyes seemed to gleam with a fierce joy, and every muscle became tense with the fire that burned within. And when he led a regiment or brigade to the charge, which he sometimes did, he became the very incarnation of battle. He was 'a man of iron and fire,' enthusiastically admired by his men, almost invariably successful in his

undertakings, and one of the very few Confederate commanders who knew how to improve a victory.

He was to become the indispensible right arm of Robert E Lee, who described Jackson thus:

A man he is of contrasts so complete that he appears one day a Presbyterian deacon who delights in theological discussion and, the next, a reincarnated Joshua. He lives by the New Testament and fights by the Old.

The Shenandoah Valley of Virginia was one of the vitally important stretches of land in the Confederacy. It is the most fertile farmland imaginable, and was thus the breadbasket of the South. Beyond that, it was the ideal route for Confederate armies marching north for Maryland or Pennsylvania. To the Union the Shenandoah was strategically useless; marching south in it took them nowhere in particular. The Valley was important to the North only because it was so important to the Confederacy. Thus in October 1861 a Federal army occupied Romney, in the northern part of the Valley, and threatened Winchester; the Union was preparing to clear the Shenandoah of Confederates. In response, Stonewall Jackson and his brigade were sent to take charge of operations in the Shenandoah. With his Stonewall Brigade, some militia and other troops, Jackson (now a major-general) commanded around 10,000 men. The main Union forces in the area were some 10,000 under General Nathaniel P Banks.

After a winter of mostly fruitless maneuvering by both sides, Banks occupied Winchester in March of 1862, chasing Jackson's forces away and sending a Federal division south to occupy Strasburg. From that position Banks prepared to leave the Valley and join General McClellan's Federal Army of the Potomac, which was marching toward Richmond.

On 21 March Jackson learned of the planned Federal move from his cavalry commander Turner Ashby. It was as clear to Jackson as it was to his superiors that this must not happen: if Banks or any other major Union forces joined McClellan (a Federal army under McDowell was just east of the Valley and also slated to reinforce McClellan) they would gain overwhelming strength, and the Confederacy would be doomed. Lee, who at that time was overseeing operations in Virginia rather than commanding in the field, ordered Jackson to make a strategic diversion to keep Union forces, especially Banks' and McDowell's, in the Shenandoah and away from McClellan. In the process, he was to try and confuse the Union high command into scattering their armies and also defend Richmond from the west. In all those requirements Jackson was to prove successful beyond anyone's expectations.

Hurrying to keep the Federals in place, Jackson ordered Ashby's cavalry to attack Shields' division of Banks' army at Kernstown on 22 March 1862.

Major General John Charles Frémont USA (1813-90) commanded the Union Forces in West Virginia.

General Nathaniel Banks USA commanded a Union Army against Jackson in the Shenandoah Valley.

Next day Jackson arrived and followed up with his infantry (after searching his soul about fighting on Sunday). The Confederate attack went well for a while, until Shields moved some concealed forces into line. Then, outnumbered and low on ammunition, Jackson's men retreated precipitously, with Ashby covering the rear. Casualties in the fighting were disproportionate: the South had lost 700 of 4200 engaged; the Union 590 of 9000 engaged. It seemed a most unpromising beginning for Jackson's campaign.

In fact, Kernstown proved to be as good as a major victory for the South. Federal authorities assumed that Jackson's command was far larger than it actually was, and simply threw over the entire plan to reinforce McClellan (to that general's great disgust – for all his mistakes, McClellan understood better than his superiors in Washington that Jackson's campaign was a diversion). Orders went out from Washington: Banks and McDowell were to stay in the Shenandoah to deal with Jackson; indeed, some troops were stripped from McClellan for the purpose. At length there were three uncoordinated Federal commands trying to clear the Shenandoah Valley – Banks, McDowell, and, to the west, the army of John C Frémont.

As the Federal armies prepared to pursue him, Jackson withdrew gradually up the Valley (that is, to the south) with his 6000 men; Banks cautiously followed with 15,000. Then Jackson suddenly made a forced march to Swift Run Gap, in the eastern mountains. There his command was on the flank of

Banks' army at Harrisonburg. Banks thus could not continue on up the Valley or Jackson would be behind him, on the Union supply line. At Swift Run Gap in late April, Jackson was reinforced by 8000 men including the command of General Richard S Ewell; now his forces totalled some 17,000 (which was as great as they would become in the ensuing campaign).

Of course, the Federals were not standing still; Frémont began moving his forces east to join Banks in operating against Jackson. Learning of this, Jackson made plans to stop that conjunction, which would likely to be fatal to his efforts. As he would so often in the future, Lee wisely gave Jackson free rein. With a series of brilliant and lightning-quick maneuvers (quick for that era, at any rate), Jackson began his momentous campaign.

Leaving Ewell at Swift Run Gap to keep Banks in place and sending Ashby's cavalry to make some feinting attacks, Jackson moved to strike Frémont's advance. In the most rigorous secrecy, the Confederates began their march. General John D Imboden, on Jackson's staff, remembered the confusion of that time:

Early in May, Jackson was near Port Republic contemplating his surroundings and maturing his plans. What these latter were no one but himself knew. Suddenly the appalling news spread through the Valley that he had fled to the east side of the Blue Ridge through Brown's and Swift Run Gaps. Only Ashby remained behind . . . reporting to Jackson every movement of the enemy. Despair was fast settling upon the minds of the people of the Valley. Jackson made no concealment of his flight, the news of which soon reached his enemies, Milroy [of Banks' Union command] advanced . . . and was preparing to move his entire force to Staunton, to be followed by Frémont.

Jackson had collected . . . enough railway trains to transport all of his little army. That it was to be taken to Richmond when the troops were all embarked no one doubted. It was Sunday, and many of his sturdy soldiers were Valley men [as was Jackson]. With sad and gloomy hearts they boarded the trains . . . When all were on, lo! they took a westward course, and a little after noon the first train rolled into Staunton.

News of Jackson's arrival spread like wild-fire, and crowds flocked to the station to see the soldiers and learn what it all meant. No one knew.

Only Jackson knew that his destination was the town of McDowell, where Milroy's division was pulling in. Driving his troops in continuous forced marches, Jackson moved to the attack. So fast did his men march that they began to be called 'foot cavalry'; they made 92 miles in four days of wet and muddy weather. On 7 May they drove Federal outposts back into McDowell. There the Federal

command numbered some 6000, under Milroy and Schenck, to Jackson's 10,000. With classic skill, Jackson had maneuvered his small army to gain local superiority over his enemy.

On 8 May 1862, the Federals took the initiative at McDowell, attacking in the afternoon. Despite heavy losses, the Confederates repulsed the attack and sent the Yankees running west. Though the wet weather and enemy resistance made pursuit most difficult, the Rebels managed to chase their enemy to Franklin, West Virginia. Then Jackson withdrew, using Ashby's cavalry as a screen. The South had lost 498 men to the Union's 256, but they had won the day. Jackson, however, was by no means ready to rest.

On 14 May he marched his command for Harrisonburg. General Richard Taylor, one of Jackson's staff and son of President Zachary Taylor, painted a romantic picture of the Valley during that march of summer 1862:

The great Valley of Virginia was before us in all its beauty. Fields of wheat spread far and wide, interspersed with woodlands, bright in their robes of tender green. Wherever appropriate sites existed, quaint old mills, with turning wheels, were busily grinding the previous year's harvest; and grove and eminence showed comfortable homesteads . . . The theatre of war in this region

Frémont was relieved of his command in June 1862. In 1864 he was considered a strong contender for the Republican presidential nomination.

Right: Belle Boyd (1843-1900) served as a Confederate spy until 1864.

Below: Jackson's Foot Cavalry were a ragtail army who managed to march 30 miles in a day.

was from Staunton to the Potomac, one hundred and twenty miles, with an average width of some twenty-five miles; and the Blue Ridge and Alleghanies bounded it east and west. Drained by the Shenandoah [River] with its numerous affluents, the surface was nowhere flat, but a succession of graceful swells, occasionally rising into abrupt hills ... Frequent passes or gaps in the mountains, through which wagon roads had been constructed, afforded easy access from east and west; and pikes were excellent.

As the Confederates marched, Banks dug his army in at Strasburg and sent troops to reinforce General McDowell to the east. Thus Banks left himself with only 8000 men, a most dangerous position to be in with Stonewall Jackson around. At that point Jackson seemed, as far as the Federals were concerned, to disappear from the face of the earth. Feinting at Banks with cavalry, Jackson took the bulk of his forces east, crossed the Massanutten Mountains in the middle of the Valley, joined Ewell (making a total then of 16,000 men) and, after marching up to 30 miles a day with his 'foot cavalry,' pounced on a Federal garrison of 1000 at Front Royal on 23 May.

General Taylor remembered the approach to Front Royal:

Scarce a word was spoken on the march, as Jackson rode with me. From time to time a courier would gallop up, report, and return toward Luray. An ungraceful horseman, mounted on a sorry chestnut with a shambling gait, his huge feet with out-turned toes thrust into his stirrups, and such part of his counternance as the low visor of his shocking cap failed to conceal wearing a wooden look, our new commander was not prepossessing ...

Off the next morning, my command still in advance, and Jackson riding with me ... Past midday ... there rushed out of the wood to meet us a young, rather well-looking woman, afterward widely known as [Southern spy] Belle Boyd. Breathless with speed and agitation, some time elapsed before she found her voice. Then, with much volubility, she said we were near Front Royal, beyond the wood; that the town was filled with Federals, whose camp was on the west side of the river, where they had guns in position ... that they believed Jackson to be west of Massanutten ... that General Banks, the Federal commander, was at Winchester ... where he was slowly concentrating his widely scattered forces to meet Jackson's advance, which was expected some days later.

On 23 May Jackson struck the Federals at Front Royal. Fighting hard, the Yankees withdrew toward Strasburg; but it was hopeless – by the end of the day the Union had lost 904 of 1063 men the garrison, most of them captured. The Confederates had fewer than 50 casualties. Jackson had again concentrated to outnumber an outlying enemy detachment and won the day. Now he had to figure out what Banks was going to do next – stay put in Strasburg, go west to join Frémont, go north to strong positions at Winchester, or retreat east to safety near Washington. Deciding finally that Banks would probably stay put or go east, Jackson began marching to Middletown, near Strasburg.

Banks, for once, did not move as expected by his enemy. After learning of the disaster at Front Royal, Banks pulled his army back to Winchester, arriving on 24 May. Hearing word of the Federal move, Jackson saw its potential for trouble – knowing the area as he did, Jackson knew the town had high ground and would be impossible to assault if the Yankees settled in. So once again, he drove his 'foot cavalry' hard. At first, the exhausted Confederates dallied, wasting time looting a captured supply train. In the end, though, they marched all night and reached Winchester just after midnight.

At dawn on 25 May 1862, the Confederates drove in the Federal pickets and the battle of Winchester was on. For a time the Union cavalry and artillery kept the Rebels at bay; then Jackson put men on the Federal right flank and Ewell worked his division around to the left flank. Jackson thereupon advanced his center and right together, and the

Above: John Singleton Mosby CSA (1833-1916) served the Confederacy at the head of an 'irregular' cavalry troop which harassed the enemy.

Below: Confederate Army camps during Jackson's Valley campaign tended to be makeshift.

Federals broke and ran. Banks withdrew under pursuit across the Potomac and out of the campaign for good. Between the defeats at Front Royal and Winchester, Banks lost some 3000 men of the 8500 in his command; Jackson's losses in the same period were about 400 of 16,000.

With these extraordinary achievements under their belts, the Confederates rested a couple of days before taking the road again. They then marched north to concentrate near Harpers Ferry. One of Jackson's opponents admiringly summarized Jackson's achievements so far:

As the result of these operations, Milroy and Schenck were now beaten, Banks's army was routed, the fertile Valley of Virginia cleared of Union troops, Harpers Ferry in danger and Maryland and Washington threatened. In addition Washington was thrown into alarm and trepidation; McDowell's movement to connect with McClellan was suspended; he was ordered to move 20,000 men into the Valley to cut off Jackson, while Frémont with his whole force was ordered into the Valley at Harrisonburg for the same purpose. The whole plan of Union operations had been completely upset, and confusion reigned from one end of the line to the other. At no time during the war was there such dismay in the North ... General Jackson himself seems to have been the only one who had not lost his head. He kept his army from May 26 to May 30 threatening Harpers Ferry and an invasion of Maryland.

In deciding to devote the efforts of these commands to chasing Jackson instead of reinforcing McClellan near Richmond, the Washington authorities made one of the great blunders of the conflict, quite possibly prolonging the war for three years. All this because of the brooding, brilliant Jackson and his small band of ragged soldiers.

Of course, Jackson had planned everything to achieve just that end. But his problems were by no means over. Now he had simultaneously to keep the Federals in the Valley busy, ship east the enormous quantities of supplies he had captured, and had to pull back from the Harpers Ferry area to avoid being trapped by the converging advances of Frémont and McDowell. Leaving the Stonewall Brigade to keep Banks in check, Jackson began pulling the rest of his forces south on 30 May. Things quickly came to a head. Jackson was riding on a train in front of his

Jackson's religious faith was considered strong, even for the ardent nineteenth century.

troops when a courier stopped the engine to tell Jackson that McDowell had recaptured Front Royal. The two Federal armies were moving in faster than expected and Confederate forces were spread out around the Valley. Remaining calm in the face of final disaster, Jackson issue his orders.

The cavalry under Turner Ashby were sent to stop Frémont's advance; an infantry detachment did likewise with McDowell's men at Front Royal. By 1 June Jackson had pulled 15,000 men, 200 prisoners, and a double wagon-train seven miles long safely out of Strasburg; 50,000 Federals had not been able to corral them. Jackson then moved south up the Shenandoah Valley, burning bridges as he went. On 2 June Federal cavalry hit Jackson's rear guard, but Ashby delayed the Yankees long enough to give the Rebel infantry a day's lead. On 6 June came another Federal strike; this time the gallant Ashby was killed, but the Federal advance came to little – Union reinforcements could not move up because the Confederates had destroyed the bridges.

But by the next day Jackson was in the worst spot of the entire campaign, squarely between two converging enemy columns. With customary boldness, Jackson moved out to take the offensive from his position at Port Republic. On 7 June the Confederates tried without luck to draw Frémont out before McDowell arrived. Next morning a Federal detachment got into Port Republic and nearly captured Jackson – this was Shields' advance, part of McDowell's command moving up from the east. Meanwhile, Frémont moved to attack from the

west. It appeared to be the end of Jackson's game entirely.

Then the Federal push became muddled, mostly due, once again, to the bridges Jackson had so carefully burned. On 8 June the Federals moved

Above: Turner Ashby.

Below: An army on the march demanded food and water from the towns they moved through.

forward at Cross Keys, but were driven back and pursued; in that action, Ewell's division of 6500 bested Frémont's 10,500. On the next day Jackson held Frémont at bay with Ewell and moved to attack Shields' 3000 men at Port Republic.

On the morning of 9 June, the Stonewall Brigade hit the Federal right while others attacked the enemy left. But the Confederate efforts were driven back, and Ewell was slow to move over in support. Richard Taylor recalled his commander in the heat of this critical moment at Port Republic:

Federal lines, their right touching the river, were advancing steadily, with banners flying and arms gleaming in the sun. A gallant show, they came

on. Winder's and another brigade, with a battery, opposed them. This small force was suffering cruelly ... Below, Ewell was hurrying his men over the bridge, but it looked as if we should be doubled up on him ere he could cross and develop much strength.

Jackson was on the road, a little in advance of his line, where the fire was hottest, with reins on his horse's neck, seemingly in prayer. Attracted by my approach, he said, in his usual voice, 'Delightful excitement.' I replied that it was pleasant to learn he was enjoying himself, but thought he might have an indigestion of such fun if the six-gun battery [in front of them] was not silenced.

General George Stoneman USA and his staff camped near Fair Oaks, Virginia.

Ewell's advance was sent on an envelopment of the Federal left; this failed too, but then the rest of Ewell's men came up. Taylor remembered then what happened:

Wheeling to the right, with colors advanced, like a solid wall [the enemy] marched straight upon us. There seemed nothing left but to set our backs to the mountain and die hard. At the instant, crashing through the underwood, came Ewell, outriding staff and escort. He produced the effect of a reinforcement, and was welcomed with cheers. The line before us halted and threw forward skirmishers. A moment later, a shell came shrieking along it, loud Confederate cheers reached our delighted ears, and Jackson, freed from his toils, rushed up like a whirlwind, the enemy in rapid retreat.

Shields and his outnumbered Federal forces retreated in good order, fighting as they went. Frémont had been unable to help due to yet another burned bridge. In two days of battle Frémont had lost 684 casualties of 17,000 engaged; at Port Republic the Federals lost 1018. The total Southern casualties were about 1100 of 16,000 engaged. Jackson had once again defeated his enemy in detail,

Bands of irregular cavalry continually harassed the Union Forces.

Far left: Many Confederates were excellent shos.

Below: Jackson's Foot Cavalry traveled with only a bedroll and one day's rations.

Above: Both sides used abandoned houses for hospitals.

Opposite: Jackson's Valley Campaign saved the agricultural heartland of the South from destruction by the Union Forces.

one division at a time. In fact, in a month of campaigning against vastly superior total Federal forces he had outnumbered his enemy in nearly every individual engagement.

His extraordinary campaign in the Shenandoah Valley completed, the entire Federal war effort in turmoil and confusion, Jackson now marched west, to join Lee in the Seven Days Battles and the Second Manassas. In one month Jackson's army had marched more than 250 miles, fought four pitched battles and endless skirmishes, and had captured more than 400 prisoners and enormous quantities of arms and supplies. Jackson had brilliantly followed his own maxims of war:

Always mystify, mislead, and surprise the enemy, if possible; and when you strike and overcome him, never let up in the pursuit so long as your men have strength to follow; for an army routed,

if hotly pursued, becomes panick-stricken, and can then be destroyed by half their number. The other rule is, never fight against heavy odds, if by any possible maneuvering you can hurl your own force on only a part, and that the weakest part, of your enemy and crush it. Such tactics will win every time, and a small army may thus destroy a large one in detail, and repeated victory will make it invincible.

Stonewall Jackson's tactics of speed and secrecy have been studied by military men ever since (for example, these lessons were not lost on the Nazis in preparing their *Blitzkrieg* of World War II). But the immediate effect on Southern fortunes in the Civil War was direct and profound. Jackson had played a remarkable chess game and had checkmated his enemy. Now the impetus of the war in the Eastern Theater was firmly on the Confederate side.

CHAPTER IV

THE BATTLE OF
IRONCLADS

Previous spread: The battle between the *Monitor* and the *Merrimac* changed naval history forever.

Right: The James River meets Chesapeake Bay at Hampton Roads, off Norfolk, Virginia.

When war broke out the Confederacy had a number of experienced naval officers in the ranks, but very few seamen and practically no ships. Confederate Secretary of the Navy Stephen R Mallory arrived well prepared for his job; as a US Senator before the war he had been chairman of the Naval Affairs committee, and in that post had supervised modernization of the nation's fleet. As a cabinet officer in 1861, Mallory faced the prospect of building a fleet virtually out of nothing – the South seriously lacked the necessary industrial and shipbuilding facilities. Mallory moved quickly to purchase ships from abroad and to contract for building new ones in England and elsewhere. Among the most important requirements were ships that could run the Union naval blockade; a fleet of fast, sleek steamships painted black and burning smokeless coal were soon built and in service, slipping in and out of Southern ports at night.

Mallory's particular interest was new aspects of naval warfare. Over the course of the war Con-federate maritime experiments ran from the disastrous (such as submarines that proved more dangerous to their crews than to the enemy) to the very successful (the first effective moored mines in warfare). The most far-reaching brainchild of Mallory, however, was his project for building an ironclad battleship.

In 1861 there were only two lightly-armored battleships in the world, one British and one French. These ships had seen scant service in battle, and foreign governments seemed little interested in developing armored vessels. For the Confederacy, however, such ships promised a much-needed edge in naval warfare. Expedited by Mallory, the project began with a salvage job – in summer 1861 the Union frigate *Merrimack* was raised from the Gosport Navy Yard, which had been abandoned by the Federals and burned by the Confederates. The ship was cut down to the berth deck and radically rebuilt according to the design of Commander John M Brooke. Over the 170 feet of the midship section

FORTRESS MONROE, VA. AND ITS VICINITY

J. Wells. del.

R. Hinshelwood s

1 Old Point Comfort	5 Rip Raps	9 Elizabeth River
2 Fortress Monroe	6 Chesapeake Bay	10 Norfolk
3 Water Battery	7 Sewall's Point	11 Portsmouth
4 Hampton Roads	8 Craney Island	12 Dismal Swamp

13 Atlantic Ocean	17 Newport News
14 Cape Hatteras, N C	18 Hampton
15 Nansemond River	19 Mill Creek
16 James River	20 Land approach to Fortress

(the whole ship was 260 feet long) a roof of pine and oak, 24 inches thick, was built at an angle of 45 degrees. Both ends of this shield were rounded. The wood backing was then covered with armor – two layers of iron plates two inches thick and eight inches wide. From the front of the ship projected a ramming prow of cast iron. The power came from the *Merrimack*'s original two 600-horsepower steam engines, which had in fact been condemned by the Union before the ship was sunk. This resulted in a most underpowered vessel; that fact, combined with its excessive 22 feet of draught, meant that the ship could make only about four knots. Beyond that, its steering was so cumbersome that it required a half hour to turn around; a Southern navy man described her as being 'as hard to maneuver as Noah's ark.' Its crew of 350, under Commodore Franklin Buchanan, were largely untried. The gun crews, manning four rifled guns and six smoothbores, were hardly more experienced. Afloat, with her decks awash and the sloping tallow-greased iron citadel projecting, she looked rather silly, something like a floating barn roof.

Despite these problems, however, everyone knew perfectly well that this ship, if it could manage to steam into battle at all, could take on any wooden vessel afloat. This fact was not lost on the Union Navy Department. When news of the building of the Confederate ironclad made its way to Washington in August 1861, the North hastened to begin its own project for an ironclad. Among several prototype projects, the most radical one quickly garnered most of the attention. It was the design of a Swedish-born engineer named John Ericsson – a hull flat on top, covered with iron plates and rising only a couple of feet above the water, an armored pilothouse in front, and in the middle a heavily-armored rotating iron turret nine feet high (the direct ancestor of modern ship turrets). Although this turret was armed only with two large, bottle-shaped Dahlgren

The nine-foot high turret was the most distinguishing feature of the *Monitor*.

John Ericsson (1803-89), designer of the *Monitor*, developed the screw propeller for steam vessels.

Right: The angled sides of the *Merrimac*'s superstructure were covered with two-inch iron plate.

The Confederate Navy of gunboats and blockade runners were armed with captured weapons.

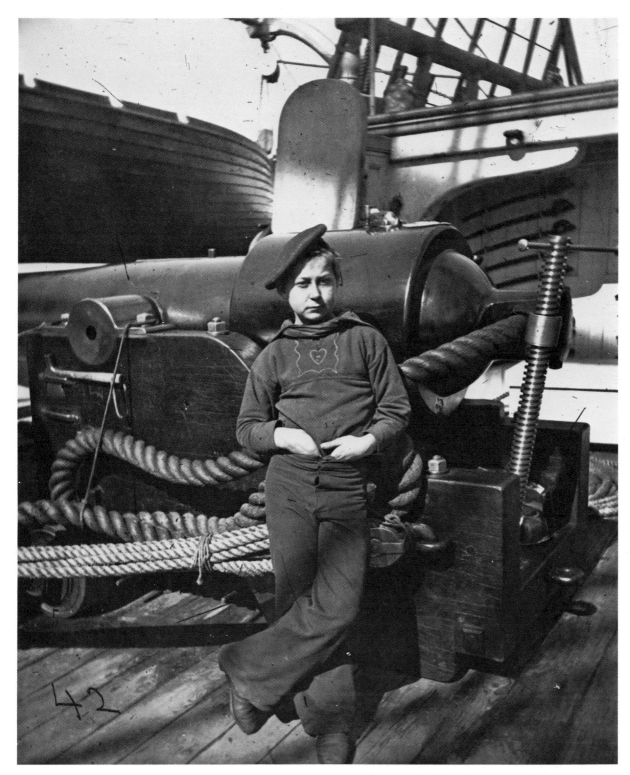

Above: Confederate sailors wore uniforms similar to those worn in the Union Navy.

Left: Small boys on both sides went to sea as 'powder monkeys.'

smoothbore cannons, the rotating feature enabled the ship to shoot in almost any direction. Christened the *Monitor*, her keel was laid on 25 October 1861, and she was launched on 30 January 1862. Her captain was Lieutenant Lorimer Worden and she carried a crew of 58 experienced sailors.

The Union's haste proved to be most fortunate, for at just about that time the Confederate's ironclad was going into action. The *Merrimack* had been rechristened the CSS *Virginia* before her launching on 30 January 1862. But the happenstance of history has persisted in calling the ship by her original US Navy name, and a misspelled form at that; so she is best identified as the *Merrimac*.

At one o'clock in the afternoon of 8 March 1862, a new age of naval warfare began. On that day the *Merrimac*, accompanied by two small gunboats, lumbered into view at Hampton Roads, Virginia, on the James River near Norfolk. In the area were 16 vessels of the Union blockading fleet, carrying some 298 guns. The Federals had been expecting the *Merrimac* for weeks, and were ready for battle. Or so they thought. The *Merrimac* made straight for the Union frigate *Cumberland* as the USS *Congress* opened a massive broadside on the Rebel ironclad. Soon the *Merrimac* was under fire from both Federal ships and from the shore. Within a few minutes the Northern gunners made a horrifying discovery: the

The USS *Cumberland* sank rapidly under the bombardment of the *Merrimac*.

Merrimac could turn away cannonballs as if they were marbles striking a brick wall. An invulnerable iron monster had stalked into the midst of wooden ships that still fought much as ships had in the fifteenth century.

The *Merrimac* rammed directly into the *Cumberland*, breaking off the ironclad's beak but nonetheless opening a yawning hole in the Federal ship. The *Cumberland* began to sink while the *Merrimac* peppered her with shell. Meanwhile, the accompanying Southern gunboats turned their cannons on the *Congress*, to great effect. Suffering heavy casualties and in flames, the *Congress* soon surren-

dered. While trying to help, three Union steam frigates ran aground.

It had been more a massacre than a battle. The *Merrimac* had taken enough broadsides to tear most ships apart, and was hardly scratched. However, the Confederate captain, Buchanan, had been injured and Lieutenant Catesby Roger Jones took command of the *Merrimac* (Jones had superintended the ship's armaments). As the ironclad retired the Rebel sailors looked forward to wreaking havoc on the Federal fleet the next day.

News of the battle brought consternation to Washington next morning. President Lincoln

headed for the Federal ships were her escort, her officers saw a strange object slip around the bow of the grounded USS *Minnesota* and head directly for them. At first Confederates took it for a boiler going for repairs on a raft; its first shot, about nine in the morning, was thought to be an accidental explosion on the raft. It was, of course, the *Monitor*. The world's first battle of ironclads, and the beginning of the modern naval age, was about to begin.

The *Monitor* steered straight for the *Merrimac*; the two Southern escorting ships dropped back like seconds at a duel. So tiny was the Union ironclad in comparison to her foe that she looked like a rat attacking an alligator. The *Merrimac* stopped her engines and waited as the *Monitor* sailed toward her starboard bow. Then the Southern ship erupted in roar and smoke, pouring a full broadside of solid shot into the enemy. The hundreds of spectators on shore and water saw both ships disappear in smoke. After an anxious moment the smoke cleared to reveal the *Monitor* unharmed; her first answering fire exploded from the turret. Inside the Rebel ship a sailor swore, 'Damn it! The thing is full of guns!' A wave of cheers went up from the Union spectators.

Reserving fire, the *Monitor* continued her approach until she was within a few yards of the *Merrimac* on a parallel but opposite course. From that distance both ships traded a devastating barrage – to virtually no effect. Finding his ship weathering the fire nicely, the Federal captain, Worden turned her about and returned to close quarters, advancing until his bow was nuzzling the sides of the enemy ship. Nothing like this had ever been seen in

The *Cumberland* returned fire which literally bounced off the armor-clad sides of the *Merrimac*.

chaired a tumultuous Cabinet meeting: Secretary of War Stanton paced the floor in a panic, proclaiming, 'Likely her first move will be to come up the Potomac and disperse Congress, destroy the Capitol and public buildings . . . Not unlikely we shall have a shell . . . in the White House before we leave this room.' The President anxiously moved to the window to search the Potomac for the approach of the *Merrimac*. (The North did not realize the ironclad's 22-foot draught would have made this impossible.)

On that same morning of 9 March the *Merrimac* moved out for the kill at Hampton Roads. But as she

history: two ships bobbing within a few feet of one another and dispensing at point-blank range the most racking fire that modern armaments were capable of, and still there was no serious damage (some shallow dents appeared in the *Monitor*'s turret and the armor of the *Merrimac* developed a few cracks).

Finding that he could not hurt the Federal vessel, Captain Jones turned his ship toward the USS *Minnesota*, receiving from that ship a broadside of 50 solid cannonballs, most of which struck square. Any wooden vessel that ever floated would have been shot to pieces; the rebel ship received the fire with impunity, and sent several shells into the *Minnesota*, with terrible effect. But before the Confederates could finish off the *Minnesota*, the *Monitor*, taking advantage of her considerably greater speed and mobility, intruded between the wooden ship and its Rebel attacker. The duel resumed between the ironclads, both sailing in wide circles seeking to find a good position to send shells into some vital part. Captain Jones tried another dash at the *Minnesota*, but this was again foiled by the *Monitor*.

As the *Monitor* crossed his bow, Captain Jones veered toward the enemy's stern and crashed into it; had the *Merrimac*'s ramming beak not been broken off the previous day, this might have damaged the Federal vessel at last. But the ramming had no effect; however, as they collided the two ships traded salvos, and a shell struck the *Monitor* pilothouse

exactly over the peephole through which Captain Worden was looking. The Federal captain fell unconscious to the floor, his face and eyes filled with powder and fragments of iron (though blinded for some days, he proved not to be seriously injured). Then the *Merrimac* turned away, receiving a cannonade into her stern that shook the Confederate ship from top to bottom. Presuming the fight would be continued, the *Monitor* dropped back to protect the *Minnesota*. But the Federals saw that the enemy ironclad was steaming away toward Norfolk. It was noon. The epochal battle was over, and neither ship had won.

Both ironclads were free of critical damage, though the *Merrimac* was sagging to the stern somewhat. The two never duelled again: for an entire month they lay watching one another, neither wishing to risk another engagement. Ironically, both ships were soon to perish outside of battle. In May 1862 the Confederates evacuated Norfolk; with her excessive draught and her unseaworthiness, the *Merrimac* could neither sail up the James to Richmond nor move to another base. There was nothing else to do but destroy the vessel. The historic ship was run ashore on 11 May 1862 and set afire. The almost equally unseaworthy *Monitor* was swamped in a gale off Cape Hatteras in December 1862 (underwater archaeologists have recently located her remains). But by the end of 1862 both navies were building more ironclads at

Despite an exchange of fire at point blank range, neither ship suffered serious damage.

top speed; the Union favoring the rotating turret of the *Monitor*, the Confederacy, the angled sides and ramming prow of the *Merrimac*.

The significance of the battle was immediately seen all over the world. A Confederate officer summarized that impact thus:

No battle was ever more widely discussed or produced a greater sensation. It revolutionized the navies of the world. Line-of-battle ships, those huge, overgrown craft, carrying from eighty to one hundred and twenty guns and from five hundred to twelve hundred men, which, from the destruction of the Spanish Armada to our time, had done most of the fighting, deciding the fate of empires, were at once universally condemned as out of date. Rams and ironclads were in future to decide all naval warfare. In this battle old things passed away, and the experience of a thousand years of battle and breeze was forgotten. The naval supremacy of England vanished in the smoke of this fight . . . The effect of the news was best described by *The Times* of London which said: 'Whereas we had available for immediate purposes one hundred and forty-nine first-class warships, we have now two, these two being the [armored] *Warrior* and her sister *Ironside*. There is not now a ship in the English navy apart from these two that it would not be madness to trust to an engagement with that little *Monitor*.'

Top: The Confederacy continued building armored gunboats similar in design to *Merrimac*.

Above: Less than a year after the battle with the *Merrimac*, USS *Monitor* foundered off Cape Hatteras.

Left: A contemporary view of the battle shows observers on both sides and the sinking *Cumberland*.

CHAPTER V

ANTIETAM

On 3 September 1862, Robert E Lee wrote President Jefferson Davis that he felt the time was right to invade Maryland. In approving the plan Davis fell prey to the same overconfidence that was affecting Lee. The confidence came, naturally enough, as the result of a brilliant series of campaigns in Virginia – the two battles of Manassas, the Seven Days and Jackson's Shenandoah Valley Campaign. It seemed to the Confederate leaders that the North was incapable of resisting Southern generalship and fighting power, and thus now was the time to take the strategic offensive, to strike the enemy in his own territory.

There were some important things Lee hoped to gain by a campaign into Maryland. He expected a good many Marylanders to rally to the Confederate flag; perhaps he could even galvanize the state into secession. Too, the invasion would indirectly threaten Washington, would keep Union forces out of Lee's beloved state of Virginia and hamstring Union military operations in all the theaters of the war. Perhaps most importantly, a successful offensive into the North might clinch ongoing efforts to gain recognition of the Confederacy from abroad; if achieved, such foreign recognition could bring vast resources of weapons and supplies to the South.

The 50,000 men of the Confederate Army of Northern Virginia waded across the Potomac River into Maryland in early September, 1862. As they marched, many of the soldiers sang the popular tune, 'Maryland, My Maryland.' Moving to shadow the invasion – moving slowly and cautiously as always – were General George B McClellan and his Union Army of the Potomac. The two actors in a great drama were thus preparing for the most devastating single day of the Civil War.

As Lee's army marched through Maryland, the local people were shocked at the ragged appearance of this dreaded band of conquerors. Unlike the comparatively grand accoutrements of the Federal army, the Rebels wore whatever they could get, which was rarely official issue of standard gray. Many wore homespun shirts, others sported captured Federal uniforms; these were sometimes dyed with walnut shells to a yellowish or butternut hue. The most common headgear (almost no one went bareheaded in this era) was not the regulation forage cap but rather a wide-brim slouch hat of felt, such as many of the men would wear on the fields of their farms at home. A toothbrush was carried in hat or buttonhole, a tin cup hung from the belt, and tied over the shoulders was the blanket, which contained a few other personal items – a pack of cards (often discarded before battle in a fit of piety), a Bible, or similar sacred and secular diversions. Shoes were in short supply in the South throughout the war; many soldiers marched and fought barefoot.

Far right: Robert Edward Lee CSA (1807-70), Commander of the Confederate Forces, was a general of almost mythic reputation.

Below: The Confederate Cavalry also served as scouts for the infantry.

Besides these practical necessities there was, of course, the fighting wherewithal – the cartridge box, bayonet, and firearm. In the beginning of the war the latter were often ancient flintlocks, newer muskets, or shotguns brought from home. Before long the Confederacy secured foreign and domestic sources of new arms and provided its army with rifled guns (another source was Union dead and captured). These rifles had spiral grooves to spin the bullet in flight, giving it a much more accurate trajectory than smoothbores could attain and thereby considerably extending the range at which accurate fire could be maintained. For the first half of the war the generals fought with Napoleonic tactics based on the charge and the standup battle; but these oldfashioned battles were being fought with modern and much more devastating weapons; thus the extraordinary high casualty figures of the war.

Another factor contributing to the casualties was the Minié bullet – the 'minnie ball' of legend. A heavy lead bullet designed to expand into the grooves of the rifling when the charge was ignited (usually by a percussion cap much like those on a modern toy gun), it caused worse wounds than did most projectiles used in the twentieth century. Any bullet that struck bone on a limb usually led to an amputation, and wounds to the body were often

fatal – a direct hit could blow a fist-sized hole right through a man. When wounded, Civil War soldiers were at the mercy of medical science little more advanced than that of the Middle Ages; an average of one out of seven wounded men died, as compared to the one out of 50 of the Korean War. And since modern understanding of nutrition and sanitation were undeveloped, more than twice as many soldiers died from disease as from battle. In sum: virtually modern firepower combined with oldfashioned field tactics and medicine made for a grim prospect indeed for the soldiers of the day.

But as Lee's men marched in September of 1862 they were jubilant in spite of their hunger and exhaustion. As his men moved toward concentration at Frederick, Maryland, Lee issued strict orders against foraging from civilians, though many a hungry soldier showed up at the doorsteps of Marylanders begging for food. The number of stragglers was alarming, some 20,000 by Longstreet's estimation. This straggling was mainly due to the lack of good shoes and an epidemic of diarrhea aggravated by green corn and green apples from the roadside, on which many of the men had to subsist (Lee never paid proper attention to food and clothing for his army). Another problem revealed itself before long: despite many previous signs and rumors of Con-

Medical treatment during the Civil War was still in a primitive stage of development. Amputation was the usual procedure for any wound to an arm or leg.

Above: The Zouave uniform, adapted from the French, was popular in the early days of the Confederacy.

Right: McClellan's careful deployment of troops and natural caution were wasted against an army commanded by a supreme tactician like Lee.

split into several parts; detachments were ordered to take the Federal garrison at Harpers Ferry, near the entrance to the Shenandoah Valley. At Middletown, Longstreet's command turned off to the right and marched for Hagerstown. General McLaws turned left and headed almost south to cover Harpers Ferry from the north. Jackson went straight ahead, also toward Harpers Ferry by way of Martinsburg, where a Federal garrison pulled out at his approach. After taking Harpers Ferry, Jackson and McLaws were to rejoin Lee. D H Hill was left with a few men to guard the pass at South Mountain.

This is not the first time we have seen Lee violate the old military maxim that forbids dividing forces in the face of the enemy; he had done so with great success at Second Manassas and was to have his greatest triumph with this strategy at Chancellorsville. But this time the move was done in enemy territory, and with an army reduced by sickness and straggling. Longstreet argued strongly against the plan, but Lee overruled him. Soon, however, a mysterious quirk of fate nearly lost Lee his army, and the South the war, before he could take the initiative against McClellan. A Federal private recalled his astonishing discovery of 13 September:

Company F, 27th Indiana, was placed on the skirmish line and reached the suburbs of Frederick. We threw ourselves upon the grass to rest. While lying there, I noticed a large envelope. It was not sealed and when I picked it up two cigars and a paper fell out.

The cigars were readily divided and, while the needed match was being secured, I began to read the enclosed document, As I read, each line became more interesting. It was Lee's order to his army giving his plans for the next four days from that time and, if true, was exceedingly important. I carried it back to . . . the colonel. He was at that time talking to General Nathan Kimball. They read it with the same surprise which I had felt and immediately started with it to General McClellan.

This order made known not only Lee's position, but his intent. It showed that Lee had proposed to divide his army on the tenth, and that, at this time, the thirteenth, it was really separated into five divisions, and that three divisions were far away, out to capture Harpers Ferry.

At that time, McClellan's Army of the Potomac was concentrated and ready to strike. After confirming the authenticity of the order, McClellan crowed, 'Here is a paper with which, if I cannot whip Bobby Lee, I will be willing to go home!' It was the purest gold of all conceivable opportunities.

No one ever figured out who lost the order; none stepped forward to own up to such a monumental blunder. By nightfall Lee had learned from Jeb Stuart that the enemy had the order and thereby knew as much about his dispositions as he did.

federate sympathizers in Maryland, the welcome for the invading army was distinctly chilly, and Lee's efforts to recruit new soldiers came to little.

Yet the army moved, the invasion went forward, though Longstreet and others increasingly doubted the prospects of the campaign. Indeed, it was a most dangerous and ill-omened gamble that Lee was taking in marching his army into enemy territory. On 9 September he compounded that danger by issuing Special Order No. 191, directing his army to

We kept up the fight until nearly night; but late in the evening the enemy forced the pass by flanking and fighting, with overwhelming numbers, and compelled our little force to retire. To observe the caution with which the Yankees, with their vastly superior numbers, approached the mountain put one very much in mind of a lion, king of the forest, making exceedingly careful preparation to spring on a plucky little mouse. For we had only about three hundred men actually engaged . . .

As usual, correspondents of Northern newspapers will say that a little band heroic Union patriots gallantly cleaned out Crampton's Gap, defended by an overwhelming force of Rebels strongly posted and standing so thick that they had to crawl over each other to get away.

On the same day there was a similar action at South Mountain, where the Federals drove D H Hill's division out of a pass. The Army of the Potomac was now moving in with unaccustomed speed, Jackson was delayed at Harpers Ferry, and McClellan still had his chance to interpose between Lee's divided army. Things looked about as bad as they possibly could have for the South.

Learning that Jackson had finally taken Harpers Ferry, Lee made the most audacious decision of his career: he elected to stand and fight McClellan at Sharpsburg, on Antietam Creek. On that day, 15 September, he had with him 19,000 men; if and when his scattered detachments arrived, he would

Left: General Ambrose Powell Hill CSA (1825-65) was promoted to Major-General in May 1862.

The Army of Northern Virginia was deployed parallel to the Potomac River.

Realizing that with only a modicum of dispatch McClellan could strike his army and defeat it in detail, Lee hastily ordered his forces to rejoin. Meanwhile, McClellan began to move his army west – faster than usual, but not quite fast enough to fully capitalize on his opportunity.

For the South, everything depended on Jackson's speed in capturing Harpers Ferry and rejoining Lee. That operation proved to be more time-consuming than expected. Jackson arrived at the Federal garrison on the 13th, a day later than planned. A P Hill drove the Federals from the heights. That general had quarreled with Jackson and was nominally under arrest at the time; nonetheless, Jackson had restored the hard-fighting Hill to command for the present, and that decision was to save the Confederacy within the week (though he regained his command, A P Hill was to despise Jackson for arresting him until his own death in 1865). With considerable difficulty, Jackson got his artillery into position on the heights and began shelling Harpers Ferry; it took just an hour for the garrison of 12,000 to surrender (1300 Federal cavalry fought their way out during the night).

The day before, 14 September, there were two small battles involving other divisions. General McLaws, trying to get into position at Harpers Ferry, found Yankees in his rear at Crampton's Gap and had to turn to deal with them. A Southern soldier remembered the fighting:

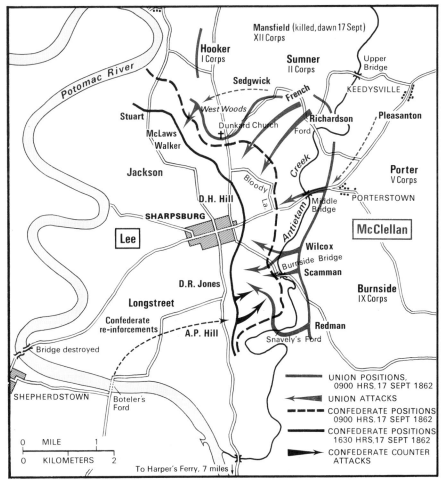

UNION POSITIONS, 0900 HRS, 17 SEPT 1862
UNION ATTACKS
CONFEDERATE POSITIONS 0900 HRS, 17 SEPT 1862
CONFEDERATE POSITIONS 1630 HRS, 17 SEPT 1862
CONFEDERATE COUNTER ATTACKS

have a total of some 52,000. The Army of Northern Virginia would then fight with the Potomac River at its back, facing an enemy army a third larger and possessing superior artillery. This extraordinary gamble, wagered with his entire army, can perhaps be best explained as an indication of Lee's exaggerated confidence in his own soldiers, combined with a quite justified estimation of McClellan's lack of fight. What Lee did not calculate, however, was that the men of the Army of the Potomac were to prove better soldiers than their leaders.

The town of Sharpsburg lay in a bend of the Potomac, with the little Antietam Creek meandering through woods, orchards and grainfields to the west. Lee began positioning his forces between the creek and the town. On 15 and 16 September McClellan moved his army to the east bank of the creek. General Longstreet later wrote of the appearance of the Army of the Potomac:

On the forenoon of the 15th, the blue uniforms of the Federals appeared among the trees that crowned the heights on the eastern bank of the Antietam. The number increased, and larger and larger grew the field of blue until it seemed to stretch as far as the eye could see, and from the tops of the mountains down to the edges of the stream gathered the great army of McClellan. It was an awe-inspiring spectacle as this grand force settled down in sight of the Confederates, then shattered by battles and scattered by long and tiresome marches.

But McClellan remained true to form: on 16 September he squandered another bit of his series of opportunities by spending the day positioning his forces instead of mounting an attack before Jackson arrived. General John G Walker noted the extra-

ordinary calm of Robert E Lee at this moment of crisis:

A little past the hour of noon on the 16th . . . General 'Stonewall' Jackson and myself reached General Lee's headquarters at Sharpsburg and reported the arrival of our commands . . . The thought of General Lee's perilous situation, with the Potomac River in his rear, confronting, with his small force, McClellan's vast army, had haunted me through the long hours of the night's march, and I expected to find General Lee anxious and careworn. Anxious enough, no doubt, he was; but there was nothing in his look or manner to indicate it. On the contrary, he was calm, dignified, and even cheerful. If he had had a well-equipped army of a hundred thousand veterans at his back, he could not have appeared more composed and confident.

At that point, the divisions of R H Anderson, McLaws and A P Hill had yet to arrive. Lee positioned Jackson to the left of his line, D H Hill in the center, Longstreet on the right, and Walker's division in reserve. In the evening of the 16th General John B Hood's Rebel divisions skirmished with General Joseph Hooker's men around a little white brick church in the center of the lines. Then the Confederates bivouacked and waited for the inevitable attack on the morrow.

In following the confused course of that day's action, it is useful to keep in mind these observations concerning soldiers in battle that were written later by a participant:

It is astonishing how soon, and by what slight causes, regularity of formation and movement are lost in actual battle. Disintegration begins with the first shot. To the book-soldier all order seems destroyed, months of drill apparently going for nothing in a few minutes. Next after the most powerful factor in the derangement – the enemy – come natural obstacles and the inequalities of the ground. One of the commonest is a patch of trees. An advancing line lags there inevitably, the rest of the line swinging around insensibly, with the view of keeping the alignment, and so losing

Above: The battle of Antietam began with opposing artillery barrages.

Opposite top: The Confederates used a ledge of rock as a defensive position.

Opposite middle: Confederate troops took cover in a cornfield.

Opposite bottom: The Confederates were impressed by the orderly ranks of well-dressed Union troops.

direction. The struggle for the possession of such a point is sure to be persistent. Wounded men crawl to a wood for shelter, broken troops reform behind it, a battery planted in its edge will stick there after other parts of the line have given way. Often a slight rise of ground in an open field, not noticeable a thousand yards away, becomes, in the keep of a stubborn regiment, a powerful headland against which the waves of battle roll and break, requiring new dispositions and much time to clear it. A stronger fortress than a casual railroad embankment often proves, it would be difficult to find; and as for a sunken road, what possibilities of victory or disaster lie in that obstruction . . . At Antietam it was a low, rocky ledge, prefaced by a corn-field. There were woods, too, and knolls, and there were other cornfields; but the student of that battle knows one corn-field only – *the* corn-field, now historic, lying a quarter of a mile north of Dunker Church.

The battle began at first light on 17 September 1862. First, opposing batteries rumbled into action. Surveying the landscape, the Union general, Joseph Hooker, could dimly see the little white Dunker Church on high ground beyond the cornfield, just in front of the West Woods. Hooker realized that building was the key to everything: take it, and you take the Rebel center, and Lee is finished. Hooker set his corps marching south toward that goal, centering them on the Hagerstown Turnpike. The advancing Federals quickly ran into trouble, most of it coming from within placid rows of corn in the field between the East and West Woods, where lay the Confederate left flank. General Hooker recalled the approach:

We had not proceeded far before I discovered that a heavy force of the enemy had taken possession of a corn-field (I have since learned about a thirty-acre field) in my immediate front, and from the sun's rays falling on their bayonets projecting above the corn could see that the field was filled with the enemy, with arms in their hands.

Above: Even the Confederate Army had trouble with deserters during the battle of Antietam.

A Union officer continues the narrative of the terrible moments that ensued:

I directed Sergeant Huntington to tell Captain Kellogg that he could get cover in the corn ... Huntington was struck by a bullet, but delivered the order. Kellogg ordered his men up, but so many were shot that he ordered them down again at once. While this took place on the turnpike, our companies were marching forward through the thick corn, on the right of a long line of battle ... At the front edge of the cornfield was a low Virginia rail fence. Before the corn were open fields, beyond which was a strip of woods surrounding [the Dunker Church]. As we appeared at the edge of the corn, a long line of men in butternut and gray rose up from the ground. Simultaneously, the hostile battle lines opened a tremendous fire upon each other. Men, I can not say fell; they were knocked out of the ranks by dozens. But we jumped over the fence, and pushed on, loading, firing and shouting as we advanced. There was, on the part of the men, great hysterical excitement, eagerness to go forward, and a reckless disregard of life, of every thing but victory ...

The Fourteenth Brooklyn Regiment ... came into our line, closing the awful gaps. Now is the pinch. Men and officers ... are fused into a common mass, in the frantic struggle to shoot fast. Everybody tears cartridges, loads, passes guns, or shoots. Men are falling in their places or running back into the corn. The soldier who is shooting is furious in his energy. The soldier who is shot looks around for help with an imploring agony of death in his face.

The Federals pushed forward, were repulsed, pushed forward again. Finally, almost without direction, a jumbled wave of Union forces swarmed toward the Dunker Church. The Confederate lines were thinning; Lee began stripping forces from elsewhere on his line to meet the threat to his left. At Dunker Church the Federal offensive ran head-on into a counterattack by John B Hood's Texas Brigade – their first hot meal in days had been interrupted and they were enraged and implacable. The Texans' volley struck the Union drive like a scythe running through their line; with men falling in dozens, the Federals turned and ran, pursued by Hood's men. But in turn the Confederates were met by a Union battery at Miller farm; blasted by double-shotted canister at fifty feet, the Rebel charge fell apart. Within the little area between the cornfield and the church, the South had already suffered almost 50 percent casualties; the Union casualty figure was some 2500. Yet the day's fighting had many more long and agonizing hours to go.

The next Union thrust came about seven in the morning. Union General Joseph Mansfield led his corps to the southwest in support of Hooker's stalled offensive. With little information and only vague ideas of what he was supposed to do, Mansfield moved to the edge of the cornfield and peered out, wondering who those soldiers in it were. Deciding in the confusion that the field held Union men, he ordered his command to stop firing. Two of his officers pointed out to Mansfield that the soldiers in the field wore gray; the old general had finally agreed when a more definitive answer came – a bullet in the stomach that wounded Mansfield mortally. The fighting then swept back west across the cornfield, leaving another layer of human wreckage on the bloody field. By that time, as Hooker wrote, 'every stalk of corn in the northern and greater part of the field was cut as closely as could have been done with a knife, and the slain lay in rows precisely as they had stood in their ranks a few moments before.'

A Federal brigade under General George S Greene fought their way beyond the Dunker Church and there held on before shattered and exhausted Southern resistance, which could not drive them back but kept them from pushing farther. Greene had broken through the center of the Rebel line before he came to a stop. At that point the battle could have been clinched for the Union, Lee's line broken, his army taken, the war ended. General McClellan had 24,000 fresh troops at hand; Lee was desperately looking for men to shore up his broken center. But McClellan sent no fresh troops to reinforce Greene. Hooker had been wounded and carried from the field; his corps was devastated and disorganized. The first Union drive had spent its force, leaving a ghastly harvest on the pastures of small country farms, for possession of which thousands had been maimed and killed. The next Federal push fell directly on the Confederate center.

As Southern General John B Gordon relates, Lee had anticipated this blow:

There was an ominous lull on the left. From sheer exhaustion, both sides seemed willing to rest. General Lee took advantage of the respite and rode along his line on the right and center. With

Below: General Henry W Halleck USA (1815-72).

that wonderful power which he possessed of divining the plans and purposes of his antagonist, General Lee had decided that the Union commanders's next heavy blow would fall upon our center, and we were urged to hold on at any sacrifice. My troops held the most advanced position on this part of the field, and there was no supporting line behind us ...

The anticipated assault came ... To oppose man against man was impossible, for there were four lines of blue to my one line of gray ... My men were at once directed to lie down upon the grass. Not a shot would be fired until my voice should be heard commanding 'fire!'

The stillness was literally oppressive, as this column of Union infantry moved majestically toward us. Now the front rank was within a few rods of where I stood. With all my lung power I shouted 'fire!'

Our rifles flamed and roared in the Federals' faces like a blinding blaze of lightning. The effect was appalling. The entire front line, with few exceptions, went down. Before the rear lines could recover, my exultant men were on their feet, devouring them with successive volleys.

This staggering blow had fallen on the II Corps of Union General Edwin V Sumner, like Mansfield an old, regular-army commander. His men had swept grandly through the West Wood and through Lee's center. Now the enemy had risen seemingly out of the ground and the Federals were caught in a hail of fire from three sides. General Oliver O Howard was trying desperately to dress his lines when General John Sedgwick galloped up and screamed, 'My God, Howard. You must get out of here!' By that time no one needed to be ordered: Sumner's corps melted away like a spent wave, fled under pursuit back through the woods and the cornfield. Sedgwick was shot off his horse and 2500 casualties, half the corps, remained behind. It had all taken just fifteen

minutes. Charging across the cornfield in pursuit of Sedgwick, the Rebels met a withering fire of Federal artillery from the eastern slope and came to a halt, finally reforming to drive Greene back from Dunker Church. Watching through a telescope from headquarters, a Federal officer saw

... Sumner's debris rallying behind the wood, forming in line, and returning to the combat ... The roar of ordnance continued for twenty minutes or more when, emerging from the smoke, flying in the wildest disorder, thinned and scat-

The Confederate Artillery held the line despite massive losses and lack of ammunition.

Both armies built signal towers of logs which could be seen at a distance.

tered, we saw the enemy returning to the wood from which he had advanced. Shot and shell followed with vengeful rapidity, and anon our ordered lines were seen sweeping over the disputed field to resume their position in front of the Dunker church.

This new Federal push toward the church was led by the division of General William H French, which began their advance at about nine-thirty in the morning. In four hours of fighting nearly 12,000 men had already fallen within a square some 1000 yards on a side. Now French's men were marching into one of the most harrowing engagements of the day. The advancing Federals found themselves on the crest of a slope looking downward toward a sunken lane which was bristling with D H Hill's men. It was only a rugged zigzagging country road, worn down by traffic and rain, looking like a mere ditch. History would remember it as Bloody Lane.

The Federals dressed their lines and descended toward the road. A Confederate officer remembered their approach: 'Their gleaming bayonets flashed like burnished silver in the sunlight. With the precision of step and perfect alignment of a holiday parade this magnificent array moved to the charge.' The holiday parade met a devastating volley from the road that blasted away the front rank and sent the rest flying back to the crest. There, hugging the dirt, they were torn by Southern artillery from high ground across the way. The notion of attacking the little road seemed utterly suicidal. Then more Federal divisions moved up, and the hard-fighting Irish Brigade was ordered in to meet a Confederate flank attack on the left. The opposing charges crashed into one another at point-blank range while Southern artillery opened up enfilade fire from both sides. The Irishmen decided they could do no worse than advance, and slowly pushed the Rebels back. Fresh Union troops arrived and drove past the Irishmen as they came exhausted to a halt.

Painfully, the Federals fought closer and closer to Bloody Lane. A Union officer remembered that in the heat of the fighting he suddenly found himself in that blood-drenched road:

> On looking around me I found that we were in the old, sunken road . . . and that the bed of it lay from one to three feet below the surface of the crest along which it ran. In this road there lay so many dead rebels that they formed a line which one might have walked upon as far as I could see, many of whom had been killed by the most horrible wounds of shot and shell, and they lay just as they had been killed apparently, amid the blood which was soaking the earth. It was on this ghastly flooring that we kneeled for the last struggle.

The Confederates made several charges to retake Bloody Lane, all to no avail. Once again the Southern center was teetering on the edge of ruin. Confederate forces were shot to pieces, Hood reporting his division 'dead on the field.' Longstreet, in command of the Southern center, wrote of the crisis of that hour:

> We were under the crest of a hill occupying a position that ought to have been held by from four to six brigades. The only troops there were Cooke's regiment . . . and they were without a cartridge. As I rode along the line with my staff I saw two pieces of the Washington Artillery . . . but there were not enough men to man them . . . This was a fearful situation for the Confederate

General Ambrose Everett Burnside USA (1824-81).

center. I put my staff-officers to the guns while I held their horses. It was easy to see that if the Federals broke through our line there, the Confederate army would be cut in two and probably destroyed, for we were already badly whipped and were only holding our ground by sheer force of desperation . . . We loaded up our little guns with canister and sent a rattle of hail into the Federals as they came up over the crest of the hill.

That little battery shot harder and faster, with a sort of human energy, as though it realized that it was to hold the thousands of Federals at bay or the battle was lost. So warm was the reception we gave them that they dodged back behind the crest of the hill . . . We made it lively while it lasted. In the meantime General Chilton, General Lee's chief of staff, made his way to me and asked, 'Where are the troops you are holding your line with?' I pointed to my two pieces and Cooke's

regiment, and replied, 'There they are; but that regiment hasn't a cartridge.'

Chilton's eyes popped as though they would come out of his head.

Receiving the report from Longstreet, Lee somehow found enough reinforcements to hold the Union drive at bay in his center. Longstreet later wrote that ten thousand Federals could have swamped Lee's army then and there. But once again, no reinforcements arrived from McClellan. By pulling his punch now at the thought of more carnage, McClellan thereby helped to ensure that the carnage would continue for two and one-half years more. The Army of the Potomac had been handed an astonishing series of opportunities over the last few days and its leaders had squandered them all, one by one. Now there was but one opportunity remaining for the Union; it lay on Lee's right,

The stone bridge across Antietam creek was Burnside's objective.

Following spread: Burnside's men were mowed down as they attempted to cross the bridge.

Above: General Joseph Eggleston Johnston CSA (1807-91).

Below: President Lincoln kept close watch on the Union Army in the field and would frequently join it to confer with his generals.

opposite which Federal general Ambrose E Burnside was in command. After the uncoordinated Federal attacks on the Confederate left and center, the third act of the battle was to be played out on the right.

Burnside had been spending all morning trying to get his men across a small stone bridge over the Antietam that chronicles would remember by his name. Lee had posted sharpshooters on the western bank of the creek to cover the bridge and all its approaches, and a goodly number of fieldpieces were trained on the area as well. While Burnside was occupied trying to cross the bridge Lee had been able to strip forces from that sector and gain local superiority elsewhere.

So mesmerized was Burnside by his bridge that he never discovered the Antietam was so shallow it could be waded at almost any point without wetting one's shirt. The idea of going downstream a bit and wading across simply did not occur to the be-whiskered Union commander. Therefore, Burnside was obliged to throw his troops into a narrow approach enfiladed in every inch by enemy fire. A series of attacks through the morning were easily repulsed by the Confederates. At one o'clock in the afternoon McClellan ordered the bridge taken at all costs. Covered by all the fire Burnside could muster, two Federal brigades gallantly pressed over the bridge, losing 500 men, and began to push back the Rebels on the hills beyond. Since Lee had thinned defenses there to only some 2500 infantry and a few cannons, the Union now had one last golden opportunity: envelop the Southern left and take Lee's whole army.

The bridge was broached at one o'clock. Not until three o'clock did Burnside begin a major advance, and he did with only one of the four divisions he had at hand. But still he outnumbered the Confederates, and his forces slowly pushed then back to the edge of

Sharpsburg. Advancing toward the town, driving back last-ditch Southern resistance, Union General Isaac Rodman saw a field of corn to his left. Something looked bad about that field, and Rodman tried to swing the green troops of the 16th Connecticut to face it. The brigade fell into confusion, and at just that time a murderous volley poured from the corn-field.

It came from the forces of A P Hill, who had that instant arrived after a 17-mile forced march from Harpers Ferry. To complete the Federals' confusion, these Rebels were wearing captured blue uniforms. The Yankees, a moment before dashing to final victory, were being mowed down in hundreds and could not even determine whom to shoot at. The Union attack faltered, collapsed. A P Hill, still technically under arrest at Jackson's orders, had saved the Confederacy. He would go on to fight at Lee's side until his death on the battlefield in the last days of the war. Hill's name would be among the last words both Stonewall Jackson and Robert E Lee uttered in their moment of death.

The battle of Antietam, the most devastating single day of the Civil War, was over.

For the North, there were 2108 dead, 9549 wounded, 753 missing; 12,410 casualties of 75,316 effective. The South lost 2700 dead, 9024 wounded, 2000 missing, 13,724 casualties of 51,844 effective. For both sides, the price in high-level officers alone was disastrous: Union generals Mansfield, Richard-son and Rodman were mortally wounded, Barlow, Hooker, Williams, Sedgwick and Richardson wounded as well, among others; of Lee's army, generals Jones, Lawton and Gordon were wounded, the latter five times, and the 'Stonewall' Division was nearly wrecked.

General Longstreet summed up the battle and Lee's response in the next few days:

In the afternoon of September 18, General Lee was advised of new arrivals in General McClellan's army and, thinking the few stragglers who came up to swell his own ranks were not sufficient to justify him in renewing the battle on the nineteenth, ordered his trains back, and after night marched his troops across the Potomac . . .

General McClellan's plan of the battle was not strong, the handling and execution were less so. Battles by the extreme right and left, divided by the river, gave us the benefit of interior lines, and it was this that saved the Confederate army.

Both armies were seriously damaged but would live to fight again. Lee had neither won nor lost his gamble. The outcome was manifestly a stalemate, one that left nearly 25,000 men dead and maimed.

But in the long run the North won a kind of victory. Lee had not been defeated, but his invasion had been stymied. The North, remembering the humiliations of First and Second Manassas, were content to call Antietam a great victory, and it raised Union spirits measurably. Most important of all, the battle gave Abraham Lincoln the chance he had been waiting for to release his Emancipation Proclamation, which was the beginning of the end of slavery in America. It transformed the public perception of the war from a fight against secession to a crusade against slavery. After that, no powerful European country could recognize the Confederacy without appearing to be on the side of slavery and oppression. Henceforth the South had to go it alone, and it lacked the manpower and resources to do that forever.

Lincoln was not pleased with McClellan's strategy and tactics, and dismissed him from command of the Army of the Potomac.

CHAPTER VI

FREDERICKSBURG

After the convulsion of Antietam the two great armies of the East rested, licking their wounds. Nonetheless, the processes of planning, raiding, and reconnaissance continued: in early October, Jeb Stuart and his Southern cavalrymen raided completely around the Army of the Potomac, as they had done before, during the Peninsular Campaign. President Lincoln goaded McClellan to action, and the general reluctantly put his army in motion to the south – as always, with maddening caution. Lincoln had seen it before; McClellan, Lincoln had cracked, was chronically infected with 'the slows.' This time, however, the President had had enough. Lincoln was not fooled into thinking Antietam a victory, as most of the North thought it. Now his general had returned to his inchworm mode of campaigning. On 7 November 1982, Lincoln removed McClellan from command. It was undoubtedly a long overdue change. But as McClellan's replacement Lincoln made a most unfortunate choice – General Ambrose E Burnside, who happened to be one of the most inept generals of all time.

A genial and handsome man, Burnside sported an extravagant set of muttonchop whiskers which were perhaps his most enduring legacy – they gave the word 'sideburns' to the language. Perhaps the secret of his success was that 'Burn', as he was affectionately known, *looked* the way most folks thought a general should look. Favoring the appointment as well, from the President's point of view, was the fact that Burnside had no political ambitions, as

McClellan certainly did (McClellan was to challenge Lincoln for the presidency in the next election). And Burnside's incompetent handling of his forces at the Antietam bridge was somehow interpreted as a triumph. As to Burnside's generalship – Grant wrote that he was 'an officer who was generally liked and respected. He was not, however, fitted to command an army. No one knew this better than himself.' Hearing the news of McClellan's departure, Lee mused with his gentle humor to Longstreet that he regretted to part with McClellan, 'for we always understood each other so well. I fear they may continue to make these changes till they find some one whom I don't understand.'

When Burnside assumed command, his Army of the Potomac was near Warrenton, Virginia, nearly between Jackson's and Longstreet's divisions, Jackson then being in the Shenandoah Valley and Longstreet at Culpeper. Instead of striking the two enemy wings in succession, with a fair chance of defeating them in detail, Burnside simply decided to try and make a beeline for Richmond, occupying Fredericksburg on the way. This was his first blunder: his real goal should have been to conquer Lee's army, not the Rebel capital.

On 17 November Sumner's Federal division arrived across the river from Fredericksburg, which lay on the banks of the Rappahannock. At that point Sumner could have taken the town without resistance; Longstreet's division was alerted and on the way but not yet arrived. Making his second big

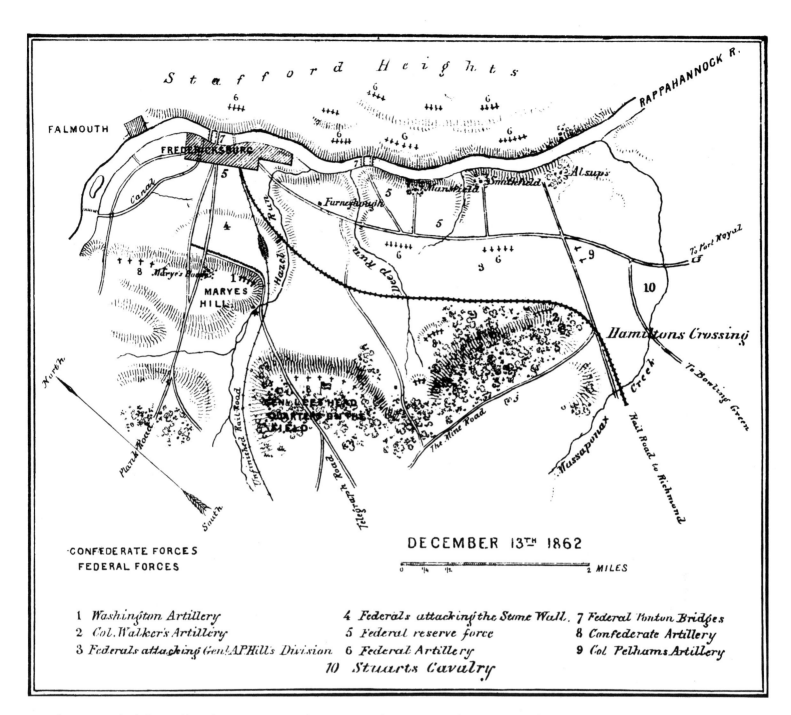

DECEMBER 13TH 1862

0   1/4   1/2   2 MILES

·CONFEDERATE FORCES
FEDERAL FORCES

1 *Washington Artillery*
2 *Col. Walker's Artillery*
3 *Federals attacking Gen! AP Hill's Division*
4 *Federals attacking the Stone Wall*
5 *Federal reserve force*
6 *Federal Artillery*
7 *Federal Ponton Bridges*
8 *Confederate Artillery*
9 *Col Pelham's Artillery*
10 *Stuarts Cavalry*

mistake, Burnside did not allow Sumner to cross the river but told him to wait for the arrival of a pontoon train with which to build bridges.

Longstreet arrived on 18 November; Jackson's corps did not pull in until the 30th. During this time, when the enemy was quite vulnerable, Burnside sat on the east bank waiting for his pontoons. Arriving on the 20th, Lee sized up his opponent with his usual acumen and decided to dig his army into the heights behind Fredericksburg, and from there to await the attack. Burnside's pontoons arrived on the 25th of November; nonetheless, he delayed his offensive until 11 December, giving the Confederates time to construct virtually invulnerable positions on high ground. Longstreet described these:

The hills occupied by the Confederate forces, although over-crowned by the heights of Stafford [on the Union side], were so distant as to be outside the range of effective fire by the Federal guns, and, with the lower receding grounds between them, formed a defensive series that may be likened to natural bastions. Taylor's Hill, on our left, was unassailable; Marye's Hill (*sic*) was more advanced toward the town, was of a gradual ascent and of less height than the others, and we considered it the point most assailable, and guarded it accordingly. The events that followed proved the correctness of our opinion on that point.

The Confederates had some 20 days to prepare for the Federal crossing and the battle. Lee had wisely picked the heights behind Fredericksburg to defend rather than the town itself. Knowing he could not prevent the Federals from crossing the Rappahannock, he positioned sharpshooters in town to slow

The heights above Fredericksburg gave the Confederate Army a great defensive advantage.

Above: The Rappahannock River acted as an additional barrier to the Union Army attacking Fredericksburg.

Below: The attack on Fredericksburg was a preliminary in Burnside's plan to capture Richmond.

the crossing. The Confederates had 78,500 men to Burnside's 122,000 – as always, Lee was vastly outnumbered. For the Southerners, it was a matter of nearly three weeks of waiting. Confederate general Lafayette McLaws recalled a striking incident of that time:

Two or three evenings previous to the Federal attempt to cross, I was with General Barksdale, and we were attracted by one or more of the enemy's bands playing at their end of the railroad

bridge. A number of their officers and a crowd of their men were about the band cheering their national airs, the 'Star Spangled Banner,' 'Hail Columbia,' and others, once so dear to us all. It seemed as if they expected some response from us, but none was given until, finally, they struck up 'Dixie,' and then both sides cheered, with much laughter.

All knew that such interludes were only comic relief in a vast tragedy, that the enemies now laughing and cheering over tunes that had once united them were soon to start killing one another again.

On 10 December General Burnside issued some confusing orders, the gist of which was that five pontoon bridges were to be pushed across the river for the crossing of the infantry. Longstreet remembered the effectiveness of the sharpshooters Lee had placed in the town:

On the morning of the 11th ... the Federals came down to the river's edge and began the construction of their bridges, when Barksdale opened fire with such effect that they were forced to retire. Again and again they made an effort to cross, but each time they were met and repulsed by the well-directed bullets of the Mississippians. This contest lasted until 1 o'clock, when the

Federals, with angry desperation, turned their whole available force of artillery on the little city, and sent down from the heights a perfect storm of shot and shell, crushing the houses with a cyclone of fiery metal . . . But, in the midst of all this fury, the little brigade of Mississippians clung to their work. At last, when I had everything in readiness, I sent a peremptory order to Barksdale to withdraw . . . before the Federals, who had by that time succeeded in landing a number of their troops. The Federals then constructed their pontoons without molestation, and during the night and the following day the grand division of Sumner passed over into Fredericksburg.

About a mile and a half below the town, where the Deep Run empties into the Rappahannock, General Franklin had been allowed without serious opposition to throw two pontoon-bridges on the 11th, and his grand division passed over . . . in front of Stonewall Jackson's corps. The 11th and 12th were thus spent by the Federals in crossing the river and preparing for battle.

During the night of the 12th, 50,000 Federals spent an uneasy bivouac around Fredericksburg, the time enlivened by a considerable amount of looting (though the valuables of the citizens had already been well picked by the Confederates after the civilians evacuated to the hills and woods). Everyone knew that the next day would see a bloody contest indeed; and many Federals were already in despair at the prospect of assaulting the heights.

Longstreet wrote of the dawn of the 13th, which he observed from his position of command on the left wing of Lee's army:

Secure on our hills, we grimly awaited the onslaught. The valley, the mountain-tops, everything was enveloped in the thickest fog, and the preparations for the fight were made as if under cover of night. The mist brought to us the sounds of the preparation for battle, but we were blind to the movements of the Federals. Suddenly, at 10 o'clock, as if the elements were taking a hand in the drama about to be enacted, the warmth of the sun brushed the mist away and revealed the mighty panorama in the valley below.

Franklin's 40,000 men, reinforced by two

Above: The Federal assault on Marye's Heights was easily repulsed by the Confederates.

Below: Confederate sharpshooters stationed within the town picked off attacking Union troops.

Above: In the Confederate Army, the standard weapon was still a percussion musket.

Below: The Federal Army made six assaults on the heights above Fredericksburg.

divisions of Hooker's grand division, were in front of Jackson's 30,000. The flags of the Federals fluttered gayly, the polished arms shone brightly in the sunlight, and the beautiful uniforms of the buoyant troops gave to the scene the air of a holiday occasion rather than the spectacle of a great army about to be thrown into the tumult of battle. From my place on Lee's Hill [the command post behind the center of the Southern lines] I could see almost every soldier Franklin had, and a splendid array it was. But off in the distance was Jackson's ragged infantry [on the right wing], and beyond was Stuart's battered cavalry, with their soiled hats and yellow butternut suits, a striking contrast to the handsomely equipped troops of the Federals.

Longstreet continues his narration of Franklin's attack on the Confederate right:

As the mist rose, the Confederates saw the movement against their right near Hamilton's Crossing. [Artillery] Major Pelham opened fire upon Franklin's command and gave him lively work, which was kept up until Jackson ordered Pelham to retire. Franklin then advanced rapidly to the hill where Jackson's troops had been stationed, feeling the woods with shot as he progressed. Silently Jackson awaited the approach of the Federals until they were within good range, and then he opened a terrific fire which threw the Federals into some confusion. The enemy again massed and advanced, pressing through a gap between Archer and Lane. This broke Jackson's line and threatened very serious trouble. The Federals who had wedged themselves in through that gap came upon Gregg's brigade, and then the severe encounter ensued in which the latter general was mortally wounded. Archer and Lane very soon received reinforcements and, rallying, joined in the counter-attack and recovered their lost ground . . . the counter-attack drove the Federals back to the railroad and beyond the reach of our guns on the left. Some of our troops following up this repulse got too far out, and were in turn much discomfited when left to the enemy's superior numbers, and were obliged to retire in poor condition. A Federal brigade advancing under cover of Deep Run was discovered at this time and attacked by regiments of Pender's and Law's brigades. Jackson's second line advancing, the Federals were forced to retire. This series of demonstrations and attacks, the partial success and final discomfiture of the Federals, constitute the hostile movements between the Confederate right and the Federal left.

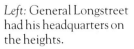

Left: General Longstreet had his headquarters on the heights.

Below: It was impossible for the Union Army to do more than struggle along at the base of the heights.

This fighting on the right had gone on for some three hours. Having been repulsed, Franklin's division sank into exhaustion, and the action shifted to the Confederate left, where Longstreet's corps lay in strongly-entrenched positions on the heights. Two days before, one of Lee's staff officers had written in his diary,

We exchanged felicitations on the great blunder of the Federal commander in preparing to attack us in a position of our own choice. Even the face of our great commander Lee, which rarely underwent any change of expression at the news of either victory or disaster, seemed to be lighted up with pleasure at every fresh report that a greater number of the enemy had crossed the river.

While the Union assaults of the 13th were breaking on Lee's right, the other half of the Army of the Potomac had been crossing the river and gathering around Fredericksburg for an all-out offensive on Longstreet's position at and below Marye's Heights. The first of six major Federal assaults set out about noon, heading straight for the strongest part of the Confederate line. Advancing across open ground, the Federal lines were torn by artillery fire, then came in rifle range of a line of Rebels, the brigade of General Thomas Cobb, posted in a sunken road behind a stone wall at the foot of Marye's Heights. A Confederate cannoneer recounted a bloody day's work on the heights:

At last the Federal line appeared above the ridge

The Confederates built
earthen fortifications at
the top of Marye's
Heights.

Above: The fighting at the Bloody Angle was responsible for many casualties.

Below: A Confederate picket at Fredericksburg kept warm in a blanket and rawhide moccasins.

in front of us and advanced. What a magnificent sight it was! It seemed like some huge blue serpent about to encompass and crush us in its folds . . . Instantly the edge of Marye's Hill (*sic*) was fringed with flame. The dreadful work of the Washington Artillery had begun. The boys aimed and fired coolly and deliberately . . . Nearer and nearer the enemy's line advanced, came within range of canister and we gave it to them. Now the Federals were near enough to the infantry in the sunken road . . . who were unseen by them . . . All at once the gray line below us rose, and volley after volley was poured into the enemy's ranks. Great gaps appeared; we gave them canister again and again; a few left the ranks – more followed; the line halted for an instant and, turning, were seen running in great disorder toward the town. The first assault had been met and repulsed. The field before us was dotted with patches of blue.

Another division now advanced in splendid style and, being joined by remnants of the first command, pushed on valiantly to and beyond the point previously reached, and then, in little more than fifteen minutes, like our first assailants was forced back. Of the 5000 men led into action 2000 fell in the charge . . . the brave fellows came within five and twenty paces of the stone wall but encountered such a fire of shot, canister and musketry as no command was ever known to live through.

From Lee's Hill, above the battlefield, Longstreet watched wave after wave of Federals advance as if on parade to be torn to pieces at the foot of Marye's Heights:

The field in front of Cobb was thickly strewn with the dead and dying Federals, but again they formed with desperate courage and renewed the attack and again were driven off. At each attack the slaughter was so great that by the time the third attack was repulsed, the ground was so thickly strewn with dead that the bodies seriously impeded the approach of the Federals.

And so it went as the long afternoon wore on, assault after hopeless and tragic assault, the Union dead and wounded piling higher before the stone wall. A Union soldier recounts one of the last assaults:

One division had just charged up the hill and, although they had failed to carry the height, hundreds of men lay prone on the ground in fair alignment, apparently too spirited to withdraw entirely from their futile effort. But a closer inspection showed all these men, hundreds in number, to be dead or too seriously wounded to move.

Our regiment still hugged the ground closely where it had first established its line. Instinctively, it began its desperate work of assault. Under the apalling musketry and amid great disorder, the advance was maintained with reasonable regularity to a brickyard, with its kiln standing, through which tore shot and shell, and

from which bricks flew in every direction. The little shelter afforded by the kiln had enticed the wounded within its reach to crawl to it for cover, and their mangled, bleeding forms lay strewn everywhere, closely packed together . . .

Someone said, 'This is awful!'

'This is what we came here for,' quietly replied our major as he dismounted.

Late in the day, as the Federal efforts were trailing off on the left, Jackson ordered an advance on the right, but he was dissuaded due to extensive Federal artillery covering the open ground in his front. Lee had shifted a number of troops from his right to the center, to meet the Union offensive, but they were scarcely necessary. As a Union soldier bitterly commented, 'No troops in the world would have won a victory if placed in the position ours were. Few armies . . . would have stood as well as ours did. It can hardly be in human nature for men to show more valor, or generals to manifest less judgment, than were perceptible on our side that day.' Another Yankee soldier put it more succinctly: 'They may as well have tried to take Hell.'

Night fell at last on the scene of carnage, and it was over for those Federals who had made their escape from Marye's Heights. But many were too wounded to move, or were trapped in front of enemy guns and hugging the ground all night. Union officer Joshua Chamberlain wrote an unforgettable account of that night of horror:

We had that costly honor which sometime falls to the 'reserve' – to go in when all is havoc and confusion, through storm and slaughter, to cover the broken and depleted ranks of comrades and take the battle from their hands. Thus we had replaced the gallant few still struggling on the crest, and received that withering fire, which nothing could withstand, by throwing ourselves flat in a slight hollow of the ground, within pistol shot of the enemy's works; and, mingled with the dead and dying that strewed the field, we returned the fire till it reddened into night, and at last fell away through darkness into silence.

But out of that silence from the battle's crash and roar rose new sounds more appalling still . . . a strange ventriloquism, of which you could not locate the source . . . a wail so far and deep and wide, as if a thousand discords were flowing together into a key-note weird, unearthly, terrible to hear and bear . . . the writhing concord broken by cries for help pierced by shrieks of paroxysm; some begging for a drop of water; some calling on God for pity; and some on friendly hands to finish what the enemy had so horribly begun; some with delirious, dreamy voices murmuring loved names, as if the dearest were bending over them . . .

At last, outwearied and depressed with the desolate scene, my own strength sunk, and I moved two dead men a little and lay down between them, making a pillow of the breast of a third. The skirt of his overcoat drawn over my face helped also to shield me from the bleak winds. There was some comfort even in this

The Federal advance at Fredericksburg has been compared to Pickett's Charge.

The Confederate Brigade of General Thomas Cobb was placed behind a stone wall at the foot of Marye's Heights and suffered accordingly.

Phot

Above: A contemporary observer described Fredericksburg after the battle as 'utterly desolate . . . before sundown a score of houses are in ashes.'

Opposite top: The Federal Army withdrew after another attempt through the winter mud.

Opposite below: The Federal casualties were greater than one in ten.

companionship . . . The deepening chill drove many forth to take the garments of those who could no longer need them, that they might keep themselves alive. More than once I was startled from my unrest by some one turning back the coat-skirt from my face, peering, half vampire-like . . . through the darkness, to discover if it too were of the silent and unresisting; turning away more disconcerted at my living word than if a voice had spoken from the dead.

In Burnside's tragic and stupid assaults of 13 December at Fredericksburg the North had lost 12,700 killed and wounded of 106,000 committed. The South's casualties were less than half those – 5300 casualties of 72,500 engaged. During the night a Federal prisoner caught in Confederate lines produced a memorandum from Burnside ordering renewed attacks next day. Lee and Longstreet made ready to meet it. The attack never came; Burnside's staff had dissuaded him. Surveying the field that showed only dead and dying Federals and no attack, Lee joked to Longstreet. 'General, I am losing confidence on your friend General Burnside.' Perhaps Lee should have ordered a counterattack; but he did not know how stricken the Federals were, and certainly he had on his mind his army's narrow

escapes in the Antietam campaign.

But Burnside was not quite done yet. He made one more effort to do his job, this time by marching the Army of the Potomac upstream to cross the Rappahannock in hopes of striking Lee's flank. But this operation began squarely in the middle of the usual January thaw, with its accompanying torrents of rain. During it the entire army nearly disappeared into an apparently bottomless sea of mud. This Mud March, as history dubbed it, was soon aborted and the bedraggled and demoralized Army of the Potomac slogged back to their camps across the river from Lee at Fredericksburg. Burnside had thus crowned a debacle with a fiasco. He was relieved at his own request on 25 January 1863.

Contemplating the horror and the incomprehensible stupidity of Fredericksburg, a compassionate Longstreet wrote perhaps the best epitaph for the Union dead:

The spectacle that we saw upon the battle-field was one of the most distressing I ever witnessed. The charges had been desperate and bloody, but utterly hopeless. I thought, as I saw the Federals come again and again to their death, that they deserved success if courage and daring could entitle soldiers to victory.

Right: The Confederate casualties were over 5000 in a force of 72,500.

Below: Confederate officer John Cooke.

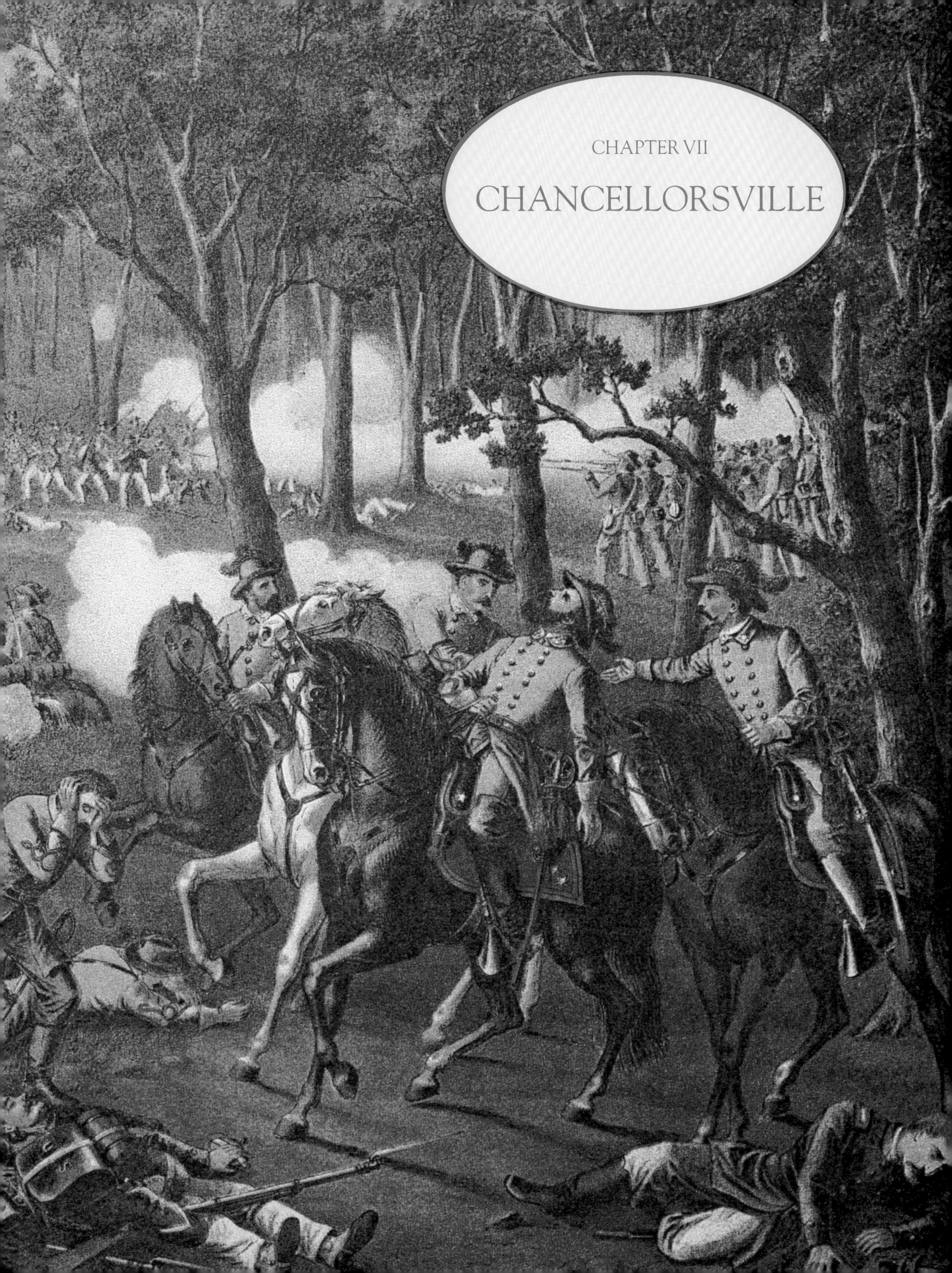

CHAPTER VII

CHANCELLORSVILLE

Previous spread: In the aftermath of Chancellorsville, Stonewall Jackson was wounded by his own men.

Opposite: The new commander of the Union Army, General Joseph Hooker (1814-79).

Below: The Army of the Potomac marched along the Rappahannock on their way to Chancellorsville.

Intelligence concerning enemies' doings traveled slowly and tenuously in the Civil War compared with later conflicts. But news always seemed to travel faster in the direction of Robert E Lee. The Confederate commander got his information from a variety of sources – above all from Jeb Stuart's cavalry, which were the eyes of the Army of Northern Virginia; from spies in Washington and in Southern towns occupied by the Union; from Northern prisoners and deserters; and, not infrequently, from reading Northern newspapers (there was little organized censorship in Washington, and often the South could find out about enemy operations simply by perusing the daily papers).

At the end of January, 1863, Lee learned that he had a new opponent, that the Union Army of the Potomac had seen the fourth change of command in a year. Following Burnside's debacle at Fredericksburg and his being relieved at his own request, Washington gave the army to General Joseph Hooker, called 'Fighting Joe' by the press. Hooker's friends in Washington had overcome political opposition to the appointment and Hooker was one of the few generals who genuinely wanted the job – indeed, he had schemed plenty to get it. Lee's response to this Federal change of command is not recorded. It is likely he knew his opponent's strengths and weaknesses as well as usual. If so, Lee knew that there were two Joe Hookers, one of them an experienced, dashing and hardfighting general, the other a man fond of criticizing his superiors and scheming for his own benefit, and equally fond of the bottle and the ladies.

But in taking command in the winter of 1863 Hooker suddenly revealed unexpected qualities as an organizer. He repaired the Army of the Potomac from the ground up, improved the food supply, hospital care, and sanitation of his troops, and drilled them incessantly. The intelligence service was reorganized with the result that there were fewer of the exaggerated estimates of Lee's strength that had plagued McClellan. The pride and morale of the army rose with its physical condition and its numbers: by April there were 122,000 infantry, 12,000 men in a well-trained cavalry, and 400 cannons. Hooker called it the greatest army on the planet, and maybe it was. Once he put his army in motion, Hooker crowed, 'May God have mercy on General Lee, for I will have none!'

In April, Lee's Army of Northern Virginia still lay along the Rappahannock at Fredericksburg. To dislodge them, Hooker devised a plan that was sound and imaginative: leaving a force to hold Lee in position, Hooker would march the bulk of his infantry around Fredericksburg in a wide strategic envelopment, crossing the river and coming in behind Lee from the west. In theory, the Confederates then had the choice of sitting and being destroyed or retreating and thus exposing their flank to the Federals.

Hooker was sure his revitalized cavalry could take on Jeb Stuart now. Thus he prepared his campaign by sending 12,000 horsemen on a raid to cut Southern supply lines in the rear. Leaving on 13 April, the Union riders soon ran into floods on the rivers that held them up for two weeks, after which

Above: A Confederate powder flask.

Right: Hooker thoroughly reorganized the Union Army.

they ranged around to little purpose. Lee sent Stuart and his scouts to investigate this floundering maneuver, and after receiving the report simply ignored the Federal cavalry.

On 27 April Hooker struck camp, leaving 40,000 men under General John Sedgwick to hold Lee in place at Fredericksburg, and moved the rest of his army northwest and then south across fords on the Rappahannock and Rapidan. By 30 April these forces were gathered around Chancellorsville, which was simply a wide clearing with a mansion

near on a road crossing. Surrounding the clearing was the virtually impenetrable forest of the Virginia Wilderness. On the 30th the Federals began marching toward Fredericksburg, ready to take the Rebels by surprise.

However, Robert E Lee had no intention of playing his assigned role in Hooker's little game. Lee and his generals had divined what Joe Hooker was going to do almost as soon as Hooker did. A Federal general recounts the information he found in a captured officer's diary:

In March a council of war had been held at General Stuart's headquarters, which had been attended by Generals Jackson, A P HIll, Ewell, and Stuart. They were in conference over five hours, and came to the decision that the next battle would be at or near Chancellorsville, and that that position must be prepared.

On 30 April Jeb Stuart notified Lee that Hooker was moving his army from Chancellorsville toward the Confederate rear. At that time Lee had available some 60,000 men, less than half his enemy's strength (Longstreet and Hood were gone foraging in Virginia with a large detachment). Nonetheless, Lee once again boldly split his army to meet the

Left: Major-General James Ewell Brown (JEB) Stuart CSA (1833-64) was the most successful cavalry commander.

GEN. HOOKER'S HEAD QUARTERS CHA

LLORVILLE MAY 1ST.

Hooker tried to choose the field of battle, but the Confederate Army had beaten him to it.

Federal threat. A screening force of 10,000 men under General Jubal Early was left to hold Sedgwick at Fredericksburg and ordered to build many fires to fool the Yankees. Lee and Stonewall Jackson marched northwest on 1 May to deal with Hooker's main body.

Hooker had seen the necessity of pushing past the dense woods of the Wilderness to meet Lee on open ground, where superior Federal artillery could have room to function and the army room to maneuver. On May Day morning the Federals pulled into open country, exactly where Hooker wanted to meet the enemy. Everything was going according to Hooker's plan; Fredericksburg lay less than a dozen miles away. Then, on high ground some two miles from Chancellorsville, around ten-thirty in the morning, Federal skirmishers ran into a line of Confederate skirmishers from Anderson's and McLaws' forces.

As one Union soldier recalled, 'There they stood facing each other, steady and silent, gazing, the one in apparent wonderment, the other in real surprise at the unexpected situation.' Soon Federal units began moving up and easily forced the Rebel skirmishers back. All that seemed necessary for the

The Union Army camped at Culpeper, Virginia.

Lee and Jackson
conferred the night
before the battle.

Robert E Lee. But Joe Hooker had no such inner strength, not by a long shot. On 1 May with the Wilderness at his back and commanding vastly superior forces, Hooker began to act like a beaten man at the first brush with Lee that had not been part of his pretty plan. After several hours of inactivity he fled back to the reassuring safety of the forest, overruling the furious protests of his staff and ordering all his forces back toward Chancellorsville to dig into the Wilderness. The significance of this retreat was not lost on the Union troops. Union general Darius N Couch remembered that grim afternoon:

> The position thus abandoned was high ground, more or less open in front, over which an army might move and artillery be used advantageously; moreover, were it left in the hands of an enemy, his batteries, established on its crest and slopes, would command the position at Chancellorsville . . .
>
> Troops were hurried into position, but the observer required no wizard to tell him, as they marched past, that the high expectations which had animated them only a few hours ago had given place to disappointment. Proceeding to the Chancellor house, I narrated my operations in front to Hooker, which were seemingly satisfactory, as he said: 'It is all right, Couch, I have got Lee just where I want him; he must fight me on my own ground.' The retrograde movement had prepared me for something of the kind, but to hear from his own lips that the advantages gained by the successful marches of his lieutenants were to culminate in fighting a defensive battle in that nest of thickets was too much, and I retired from his presence with the belief that my commanding general was a whipped man.

North was to form line of battle and sweep the Rebels back toward Fredericksburg.

For every Federal general confronting Robert E Lee, there came a moment of truth: when the full realization of just how dangerous Lee was, combined with the awful responsibility of holding in his hands the future of the American nation, came down on the Union commanding officer with the force of doom itself. That thunderclap nearly paralyzed McClellan at Antietam; it scrambled what little judgment Burnside might otherwise have had at Fredericksburg; in 1864 it would send U S Grant sobbing into his tent in the Wilderness. In the end Grant alone would have the strength to survive that terrifying revelation that came to all opponents of

Right: The Confederates charged the Union XI Corps, commanded by Colonel Oliver O Howard.

Left: The XI Corps panicked and fled before the Stonewall Brigade.

During the afternoon of 1 May Jeb Stuart's cavalry had moved freely around the Union army, and late in the day Stuart reported to Lee that the Federal right was vulnerable, 'in the air' with no real protection on the flank. A Confederate officer, Robert's nephew 'Fitz' Lee, recalled Lee's response:

On May 1 General Lee wished to cut Hooker off from the United States Ford, preventing his communication with Sedgwick, and rode down himself and examined the lands all the way to the river, but found no place where he could execute this movement. Returning at night, he found Jackson and asked him if he knew of any place to attack. Jackson said he had been inquiring about roads and soon returned with the Reverend Doctor B T Lacey, who said a circuit could be made around by the Wilderness Tavern. A young man living in the country, and then in the cavalry, was sent for to act as guide. Lee and Jackson took their seats on a log to the north side of the Plank Road and a little distant from the wood. 'General,' Lee said, 'we must get ready to attack the enemy, and you must make arrangements to move around his right flank.'

The Confederates slept on the field that night. Waking in the early morning, one of Lee's staff saw an historic meeting:

Some time after midnight I was awakened by the chill of the early morning hours, and, turning over, caught a glimpse of a little flame on the slope above me, and sitting up to see what it meant, I saw, bending over a scant fire of twigs, two men seated on old cracker boxes and warming their hands over the little fire.

It was Jackson and Lee, and they were finalizing their plans for yet another unpleasant surprise for Joe Hooker. It was to fall on that luckless Union right flank, the XI Corps. Lee would divide forces again, holding Hooker's line of some 80,000 men in place with only 12,900 Confederates while Jackson marched 30,000 around to the west to strike the exposed Federal flank.

On the morning of 2 May 1863, the Union army was well fortified and easily handled probing attacks by the Rebels. The Federals little expected that these were feints to hold them in place; still less did they realize how thin Lee's line was in their front. Meanwhile, Jackson pulled his detachment out for the march across the front of the Union army, protected by the screen of the thick woods. A Confederate officer remembers that Jackson began the march with his usual secrecy:

All was bustle and activity as I galloped along the lines on the morning of the second. Jackson's corps was marching in close columns in a direction which set us all wondering what could be his intentions, but we would as soon have thought of questioning the sagacity of our admired chief as of hesitating to follow him blindly wherever he should lead.

Thus commenced the famous flank march which, more than any other operation of the war, proved the brilliant strategical talents of General Lee and the consummate ability of his lieutenant. By about four o'clock we had completed our movement and reached a patch of wood in rear of the enemy's right wing, formed by the 11th Corps, which was encamped in a large open field not more than half a mile distant. Halting here, the cavalry threw forward a body of skirmishers to

Above: The Federal Artillery attempted to stem the tide of Jackson's advance.

Below: Major-General Daniel E Sickles USA (1825-1914).

occupy the enemy's attention, while the divisions of Jackson's corps, numbering in all about 28,000 men, moved into line of battle as fast they arrived.

Another Confederate officer observed the apparently unsuspecting Federal right flank:

Upon reaching the Plank Road some five miles west of Chancellorsville, while waiting for Stonewall to come up, I made a personal reconnaissance. What a sight presented itself to me! The soldiers were in groups, laughing, chatting, smoking, probably engaged here and there in games of cards and other amusements, feelng safe and comfortable. In the rear of them were other parties driving up and slaughtering beeves.

So impressed was I with my discovery that I rode rapidly back to the point on the Plank Road where I met Stonewall himself. 'General,' said I, 'ride with me.' He assented, and I rapidly conducted him to the point of observation. There had been no change in the picture. It was then about 2:00 P M. I watched him closely. His eyes burned with a brilliant glow, lighting up a sad face; his expression was one of intense interest; his face was colored slightly with the sense of

approaching battle and radiant at the success of his flank movement.

To my remarks he did not reply once during the five minutes he was on the hill; and yet his lips were moving.

One more look on the Federal lines, and then he rode rapidly down the hill, his arms flapping to the motions of his horse, over whose head it seemed, good rider as he was, he would certainly go.

Alas! I had looked on him for the last time.

The XI Corps was indeed ill prepared to receive Jackson, though there had actually been fair warning of his maneuver. About noon Union general Dan Sickles had noticed Jackson's force moving to his right beyond the thick woods. Hooker, wondering at first if they were in fact headed for his right flank sent a cautionary note to Howard. But then Hooker began to convince himself that Lee must be retreating; in response to all further questions Hooker spent the afternoon insisting that the Rebels were hightailing it. When Sickles asked permission to move against the enemy column in his front, Hooker agreed, apparently figuring it would hasten the enemy in their retreat. Sickles cut his way through the brush with great

Above: Expanding the limits of the battle, Hooker ordered General John Sedgwick to shell the Confederate position at Fredericksburg.

Left: A Federal battery before Fredericksburg. This time the Union Forces managed to take the heights.

difficulty and made contact with the end of the Confederate column. During the ensuing skirmish he captured some 500 men of a Georgia regiment. As these prisoners were being led to the rear, some were heard to jeer the Yanks. 'You'll catch hell before night,' and, 'You wait until Jackson gets around to your right.' (By then Jackson's column had apparently divined what their secretive commander was up to.) The Federals ignored these threats. Meanwhile Hooker stripped his right flank of Barlow's division and sent them to help Sickles pursue the supposedly retreating rebels. As Sickles pulled away he left the rest of the XI Corps isolated and even more vulnerable than before.

During the afternoon the XI Corps became nervous. Many of them were Germans who spoke little or no English. Largely for that reason they were the Cinderella outfit of the army, with an undeserved reputation for running away from battle. The rest of the men scornfully called the Eleventh the Dutchmen, and they had been put on the right to keep them out of trouble. As the afternoon wore on the men sensed something big was massing beyond the woods. Appeals began going from the front to the Corps commander, Oliver O Howard, and to Hooker's staff, asking for help; the appeals were received with derision – the enemy was certainly retreating, there was no threat whatever to the right.

At six o'clock in the afternoon the advance

positions of the XI Corps were startled to see a mass of rabbits and deer scampering out of the woods toward them. The men whooped and laughed as the animals bolted toward the rear. Then there were scattered shots and cannon suddenly appeared on the front. And then arose from thousands of throats the bone-chilling screech of the Rebel yell. Then 26,000 of Stonewall Jackson's men came crashing through the Federal flank in a front a mile wide and four divisions deep, all of them shooting and screaming like demons.

Jackson's men moved straight down the enemy trenches, the 9000 men on the XI Corps fleeing in panic before them. Amidst the rout was General Howard, 'in the middle of the roads and mounted, his maimed arm embracing a stand of colors ... while with his sound arm he was gesticulating to the men to make a stand by their flag. With bared head he was pleading with his soldiers, literally weeping as he entreated the unheeding horde.' Hooker knew nothing of the rout until he heard an aide screaming, 'My God, here they come!' A Union colonel remembered the appearance of the panic-stricken mob at Chancellorsville and the successful rally that followed:

It was a complete Bull Run rout. Men, horses, mules, rebel prisoners, wagons, guns, etc. etc. were coming down the road in terrible confusion, behind them an unceasing roar of musketry. We

Many of the contemporary Currier and Ives prints of the battle, made for the Northern market, emphasized the Union gallantry.

rode until we got into a mighty hot fire, and found that no one was attempting to make a stand, but every one running for his life . . .

I found General Hooker sitting alone on his horse in front of the Chancellor House, and delivered my message; he merely said, 'Very good, sir.' I rode back and found the Eleventh Corps still surging up the road and still this terrible roar behind them. The rebels had received no check, but now troops began to march out on the plank road and form across it.

These troops were a division of the I Corps, whom Hooker had led forward and ordered, 'Receive 'em on your bayonets!' This infantry and the XII Corps artillery shoved through the fleeing men and hit the charging Rebels obliquely, slowing their advance on the left and center. Seeing a stand of Union artillery was in danger of being overrun on the right, General Alfred Pleasonton ordered Major Peter Keenan to charge his 8th Pennsylvania Cavalry into the Rebels, to buy time to turn the guns around. Keenan cheerfully accepted the order hardly knowing it was virtually suicidal. The cavalrymen, many of them scraped up from a poker game with no idea what was happening, rode directly into the middle of the oncoming enemy. One of the surviving riders tells of that devastating charge:

Captain Corrie gave the order to draw sabers and charge. Taking a trot, we found that the road took a bend as we proceeded. When we turned the corner of the wood-road a sight met our eyes that it is impossible for me to describe. After charging over the dead men and horses of the first squadron [who had led the charge and were already riddled, Keenan going down with 13 bullets in his body], we charged into Jackson's column, and, as luck would have it, found them with empty guns – thanks to our poor comrades ahead. The enemy were as thick as bees, and we appeared to be among thousands of them in an instant.

After we reached the [Orange] Plank road we were in column of fours and on the dead run, and when we struck the enemy there occurred a 'jam' of living and dead men, friends and enemies, and horses, and the weight of the rear of our squadron broke us into utter confusion, so that at the moment every man was for himself . . .

The enemy were as much surprised as we were, and thought, no doubt, . . . that the whole cavalry corps of the Army of the Potomac was charging them. I distinctly remember hearing a number of them call out, 'I surrender, I surrender.' We did not stop to take any prisoners for fear of being captured ourselves, . . . but made for our lines as best we could.

Though scores of Union saddles were emptied, the cavalry charge gave Pleasonton time to get 22 pieces aimed into the Rebels. (Too, it was this charge that was to make the Confederates leery of

A Union force makes camp between the breastworks they have built in the Wilderness.

men on horseback that night, and this fact was soon to make for a disaster to the South.) An aide of General Pleasonton gives a vividly personal account of how those cannon, combined with the growing dusk, stopped Jackson's charge before it swamped the Union army:

General Pleasonton rode from gun to gun directing the gunners to aim low, not to get excited, to make every shot tell. [The gunners were instructed to fire into the ground at 100 yards; the canister shot would then glance from the earth and strike the oncoming enemy at about three feet. Pleasonton knew the first volley had to be devastating or the momentum of the Rebel charge would sweep them right over the battery] . . . Recovering from the disorder into which Keenan's charge had thrown them, the enemy could be seen forming line of battle in the edge of woods now in our front . . . yet such was the gloom that they could not be clearly distinguished. General Pleasonton was about to give the order to fire, when a sergeant at one of the guns said:

'General, aren't those our troops? I see our colors in the line!' [The Confederates were in fact flying captured colors, to fool the Yankees.] . . . General Pleasonton turned to me and said: 'Mr Thomson, ride out there and see who those people are.'

For myself, I was not at all curious about 'those people,' being perfectly willing to wait till they introduced themselves. Riding out between our guns, I galloped to within thirty or forty yards of them; all along the line they cried out to me, 'Come on; we're friends!' . . . I came to a halt, peering into the darkness to make sure, when a bullet whistled past me, and then came 'the rebel yell.' The line charged up the hill toward our guns, and I led it! . . . But with the report of the first shot fired at me, General Pleasonton had opened fire, and those twenty-two guns belched forth destruction at a fearfully rapid rate.

Opposite: Stonewall Jackson was promoted to Lieutenant General after Fredericksburg.

Following spread: Jackson died of pneumonia a week after his left arm was amputated during the battle.

Union wounded rest in the sun, after the battle of Chancellorsville.

Although lying down on my horse I kept an eye on the guns and guided my horse between the flashes, and in less time than it takes to tell it I was on the safe side of them. It was load and fire at will for some minutes; the enemy was mowed down in heaps; they could make no headway against such a cylcone, and ran back down the slope to the cover of the woods. But still the canister was poured into them, and a second attempt to charge the guns failed ... Old artillery officers have informed me that they never before heard such rapid firing as occurred at that engagement; the roar was a continuous one, and the execution terrific. After it had ceased I rode up to General Pleasonton and said:

'General, those people out there are rebels!'

There was a grave twinkle in his eye as he held out his hand and replied:

'Thompson, I never expected to see you again; I thought if they didn't kill you I should, but that was no time to stop for one man.'

I should have agreed with him more cordially if that one man had been somebody else.

By that time Hooker had 36 more guns pelting the enemy from Fairview Cemetary. The Rebel advance

halted before the cannonade, the troops becoming disorganized in the growing dark. Over in Hazel Grove, the 15,000 men of Sickles' III Corps had been cut off by Jackson's charge, and as night fell they began fighting their way back to their lines. After a hot and confused struggle in the gloom, with men falling from their own side's fire, part of the III Corps made it back while the rest settled into an uneasy bivouac in Hazel Grove.

Then at nine o'clock, amid the confusion of nighttime action, came the accident that was to temper this, Lee's greatest victory, with the most irreplaceable loss he ever sustained. Stonewall Jackson had ridden out scouting from his lines just west of Chancellorsville. An officer of his staff recalled the tragedy that resulted:

From the order Jackson sent to General Stuart it was evident that his intention was to storm the enemy's works as soon as the lines were formed. While these orders were issued, Jackson started slowly along the pike toward the enemy. When we had ridden only a few rods, our little party was fired upon [by a group of Union infantry], the balls passing diagonally across the pike ... At the firing our horses wheeled suddenly to the left, and General Jackson galloped away into the woods to get out of range of the bullets, but had not gone over twenty steps ere the brigade to the left of the turnpike fired a volley. It was by this fire that Jackson was wounded [by three bullets, the most serious in the left arm]. We could distinctly hear General Hill calling, at the top of his voice, to his troops to cease firing. I was alongside Jackson and saw his arm fall at his side, loosing the rein. The limb of a tree took off his cap and threw him flat on the back of his horse. I rode after him, but Jackson soon regained his seat, caught the bridle in his right hand, and turning his horse toward our men, somewhat checked his speed. I caught his horse as he reached the pike ...

I dismounted, and seeing that he was faint, I asked the General what I could do for him, or if he felt able to ride as far as into our lines. He answered, 'You had best take me down,' leaning as he spoke toward me and then falling, partially fainting from loss of blood. I caught him in my arms and held him until Captain Wynn could get his feet out of the stirrups, then we carried him a few steps and laid him on the ground.

Jackson was placed on a litter, and with his bearers came under heavy artillery fire before they could reach an ambulance. That night Jackson's left arm was amputated and he began slowly to sink. Hearing the news that Jackson had been wounded by his own troops, Lee responded prophetically, 'Jackson has lost his left arm but I have lost my right arm.'

Also during the night, Federals bivouacking near Chancellorsville heard a strange, muffled firing. It was soon discovered, to the men's horror, that the

Wilderness was burning and the woods were full of wounded; the sound was that of exploding muskets and cartridge cases. Soldiers dashed into the woods and removed the few wounded they could reach. And then the survivors sat and listened: 'Curses and yells of pain, piteous appeals and spasmodic prayers could be distinguished . . . the flames roared more fiercely, the cries grew fainter, until at last they were hushed.'

In spite of the disaster of 2 May, the next dawn brought new opportunities for the Union army, as General Couch wrote:

The situation of Jackson's corps on the morning of May 3rd was a desperate one, its front and right flank being in the presence of not far from 25,000 men, with the left flank subject to an assault of 30,000, the corps of Meade and Reynolds, by advancing them to the right, where the thicket did not present an insurmountable obstacle. It only required that Hooker should brace himself up to take a reasonable, common-sense view of the state of things, when the success gained by Jackson would have been turned into an overwhelming defeat. But Hooker became very despondent. I think that his being outgeneraled by Lee had a good deal to do with his depression.

Taking over Jackson's corps, Jeb Stuart rallied the men with the name of their stricken leader and led a savage attack at five in the morning of 3 May. Stuart caught the Federal III Corps in motion back toward their lines and pushed them out of high ground at Hazel Grove, from whence 30 Rebel cannons were brought to bear on the heart of the Federal position at Chancellorsville. The clearing around Hooker's headquarters quickly became a maelstrom of shot and shell. Then the Rebels began shoving the Federals back toward the Rappahannock.

Late on the previous evening Hooker had sent a dispatch to Sedgwick ordering him to push past the enemy at Fredericksburg and move on Lee's rear at Chancellorsville. Couch commented sourly on this order:

Some of the most anomalous occurrences of the war took place in this campaign. On the night of May 2d the commanding general, with 80,000 men in his wing of the army, directed Sedgwick, with 22,000, to march to his relief. While the officer was doing this on the 3d, and when it would be expected that every effort would be made by the right wing to do its part, only one-half of it was fought (or rather half-fought, for its ammunition was not replenished), and then the whole wing was withdrawn to a place where it could not be hurt, leaving Sedgwick to take care of himself.

That morning, 3 May, as the Confederate attack was tearing into the Union lines, Sedgwick mounted a series of assaults on Jubal Early's men at

Opposite: Federal Artillery prepares for action at Chancellorsville.

Left: Confederate prisoners brought in after the battle.

Marye's Heights, where Burnside had been so tragically repulsed in December, and finally stormed the position with heavy losses by eleven in the morning. Sedgwick then moved toward Chancellorsville, hoping to catch Lee in a vise.

On the front porch of the Chancellor mansion, his headquarters, General Hooker seemed paralyzed amidst the furious enemy fire which was destroying his batteries one by one, smashing into the house, exploding in the upper rooms and sending showers of brick fragments flying in every direction. As he stood on the front porch leaning on a pillar, straining for the sound of Sedgwick's approach, Hooker was thrown to the ground by a shell that splintered the pillar. Dazed, he gave Couch temporary command and ordered a withdrawal to entrenchments already prepared in an arc between the Rapidan and Rappahannock. The Rebels pursued this withdrawal, their cannons firing everything they could lay hands on – including old railroad iron, chains and tools. The woods burned again, consuming the dead and wounded of both sides.

As Sedgwick advanced on his rear, Lee maintained his customary calm:

A horseman was coming at full speed, and as he drew near I saw it was the chaplain of the Mississippi Brigade, and that he was greatly excited. He did not have a saddle, and his horse was reeking with sweat and panting from exertion. When his eye fell on General Lee, he made directly for him. He dashed to the very feet of the commanding general, indeed almost on him, and, gasping for breath, his eyes starting from their sockets, began to tell of dire disaster at Fredericksburg – Sedgwick had smashed Early and was rapidly coming on in our rear.

I have never seen anything more majestically calm than General Lee was. Something very like a grave sweet smile began to express itself on the general's face, but he checked it, and raising his left hand gently, he interrupted the exited speaker.

'I thank you very much,' he said, 'but both you and your horse are fatigued and overheated. Take him to that shady tree yonder and rest a little. I'll call you as soon as we are through.'

Then Lee put the finishing touch on his masterpiece. Leaving Stuart with 25,000 men to hold Hooker's dug-in 80,000, Lee marched with 20,000 men to confront Sedgwick's advance on his rear. Sedgwick ran into General Lafayette McLaws' troops around Salem Church on that afternoon of 3 May. By next morning Lee had surrounded Sedgwick on three sides with McLaws, R H Anderson, and Early, while also reoccupying Marye's Heights with William Barksdale's men. Sedgwick was driven back to Bank's Ford on the Rappahannock, where the Rebels harassed him strongly. The Federal division withdrew across the ford on the night of 4 May.

Lee began planning an all-out offensive against Hooker's remaining divisions for 6 May, an offensive that might well have been a disaster for the

South given the strength of the Federal entrenchments. Concerning this plan, Confederate general Edward P Alexander wryly commented, 'It must be conceded that Lee never in his life took a more audacious resolve than when he determined to assault Hooker's entrenchments. And it is the highest possible compliment to the army commanded by Lee to say that there were two persons who believed that, in spite of all the odds, it would have been victorious. These two persons were General Lee and General Hooker.'

But Hooker had already had enough. Over the objections of most of his staff he withdrew across the Rappahannock during the miserably wet and muddy night of 5 May. He had gone into battle with a better than two to one advantage and had nonetheless let his forces be outnumbered in every encounter; 30,000 Union troops had never been commmitted at all. A Union soldier recalled that demoralized withdrawal:

Heavens, what a retreat! We expected every moment a bloody fight, but it did not come. We wallowed through the mud up to our middles. The officers all got drunk (with a few worthy exceptions) from the general down to the line officers. The miserable fiends drew their swords and pistols, and fell off their horses, cursing. They say the Peninsular Campaign and retreat was nothing compared to this. That we should lose all and march away back to camp is enough to quench all hopes of victory!

Call it what you please, demoralization or discouragement, we cared not to sleep standing and fight running, when sure defeat always awaited such a *doomed* army.

Years later, Hooker was to make a simple confession about himself at Chancellorsville, when he confronted the battlefield genius of Lee and his army: 'To tell the truth, I just lost confidence in Joe Hooker.'

In contrast, the morale of the Army of Northern Virginia was never so exultant, their confidence in themselves and their leaders never more unshakable. But such confidence is dangerous in armies and in leaders, as the Army of Northern Virginia was about to learn once and for all. And glorious as Lee's victory at Chancellorsville was, it was a Pyrrhic one. Casualty figures are uncertain; Lee had about 12,821 in killed, missing and wounded to Union's 17,278. But while the Federals had lost 13 percent of their army, Lee had lost 22 percent of his. Numbers were beginning to count in the war; the South's supply of manpower was limited and becoming more critical with every battle won or lost.

On 10 May Stonewall Jackson cried out in delirium from his bed, 'Order A P Hill to prepare for action – pass the infantry to the front rapidly – tell Major Hawks . . .'; and then, after a silence, 'No, let us cross over the river and rest under the shade of the trees.' On that enigmatic word of peace the great warrior died.

CHAPTER VIII

GETTYSBURG

On 3 June 1863, Robert E Lee's Army of Northern Virginia pulled out of their old field of triumph at Fredericksburg, Virginia, and headed north across the Potomac, across the western edge of Maryland and into Pennsylvania. For the second time, Lee had decided to invade Union territory. He did so with an army stronger than ever – 89,000 experienced fighters, one of the most extraordinary armies in history, which had whipped the much larger and better-outfitted Union Army of the Potomac three times in the past year and fought them to a draw at Antietam. Ragged and hungry as they were, the soldiers of Lee's army were in the highest of spirits: they had the greatest general in the world and felt they were invincible. All they had to do now, they were certain, was to win just one more smashing victory and the North would let them alone at last.

But Robert E Lee knew that things were were not so good as they seemed for the South. His decision to invade the North once again was made partly in desperation. The situation in the Confederacy was critical: the Mississippi was all but lost; badly-needed European recognition had not come; the Union blockade of Southern ports was tightening, cutting off supplies from overseas; anti-war sentiment in the North was fading; Southern finances were collapsing. After much thought, Lee had concluded he had only two choices for his army.

One was to fall back on Richmond and await the inevitable siege; this course seemed to him fatal and cowardly. Lee was above all an aggressive fighter, so he chose the second option, the invasion. The only hope for the Confederacy now, Lee reasoned, was a decisive victory that would win the war in one stroke. On the desk of Jefferson Davis was a letter to be given to Lincoln after that victory, a letter from the victor to the vanquished, proposing terms for peace.

Lee knew his army would follow him anywhere, and just like his soldiers he believed they could whip anybody – their string of victories proved it. At 57 he was getting to be an old man, his heart was troubling him; he did not know how many battles he or the Confederacy had left. He must act now.

These convictions were not shared, however, by Lee's second in command, James Longstreet, whom Lee affectionately called 'my old war horse.' Longstreet objected to the invasion from the beginning, proposing instead a plan to hold Hooker and the Army of the Potomac with two divisions while sending the rest to Tennessee, where they would join Bragg and Johnston in fighting Rosecrans. This move would likely force U S Grant away from his stranglehold on the vital Southern city of Vicksburg, would paralyze the North and threaten Kentucky and Ohio. Longstreet's plan was a good one and might well have worked, but Lee rejected it.

His sights, as always, were fixed above all on his beloved Virginia; beyond his strategic decisions were deeply personal concerns – he wanted to end the Union threat to his exhausted state and find food for his army in the farms of Pennsylvania. The most Longstreet could get out of Lee was to agree that the campaign should be offensive in strategy but defensive in tactics – they must let the enemy attack them at a time and place of their own choosing. But in the end Lee would not abide by that notion either.

Before pulling out, Lee had reorganized his army into three corps with integral artillery, the corps being led by Longstreet, A P Hill, and, replacing Stonewall Jackson as best he could, the brilliant and eccentric Richard S Ewell. Longstreet objected to these appointments as well, feeling that D H Hill and Lafayette McLaws would make better corps leaders. Privately, Longstreet felt that Lee had chosen as he did because A P Hill and Ewell were Virginians; perhaps Longstreet was right about that – though he was from South Carolina.

Indeed, throughout the fateful and tragic Gettysburg Campaign that ensued in the summer of 1863, the struggle of these two men took on a tragic dimension of its own. Both were devoted to their cause, but their convictions diverged, and in that divergence lay tensions that were to have repercussions throughout the campaign.

When he headed North, Lee left A P Hill behind temporarily in order to fool Hooker. But Joe Hooker was not to be fooled this time. Union reconnaissance parties skirmished with the Rebels at Franklin's Crossing (5 June) and Brandy Station (9 June) and established that Lee was on the march. The engagement at Brandy Station was a major cavalry battle, the largest of the war. There Federal cavalry made a dawn raid into Jeb Stuart's encampments along the Rappahannock. In several hours of fierce fighting, most of it mounted, the Confederate horsemen were badly handled by Union troopers for the first time in the war, and Federal cavalry general John Buford made his reputation by leading the first charge. Stuart finally organized his forces enough to send the Yankees back across the river, but the encounter was ominous, and Southern generals recognized it as such. A Confederate officer later wrote of Brandy Station. 'One result of incalculable importance certainly did follow this battle ... it *made* the Federal cavalry. Up to that time confessedly inferior to the Southern horsemen, they gained on this day that confidence in themselves and in their commanders which enabled them to contest so fiercely the subsequent battlefields of June, July, and October.' Moreover, Brandy Station was perceived in the South as a humiliation for Jeb Stuart, who seethed with resentment, looking for a way to get his revenge with some bold stroke. Jeb Stuart, known to all as 'The Cavalier,' would soon

Below: Gettysburg became the scene of fierce fighting by sheer accident.

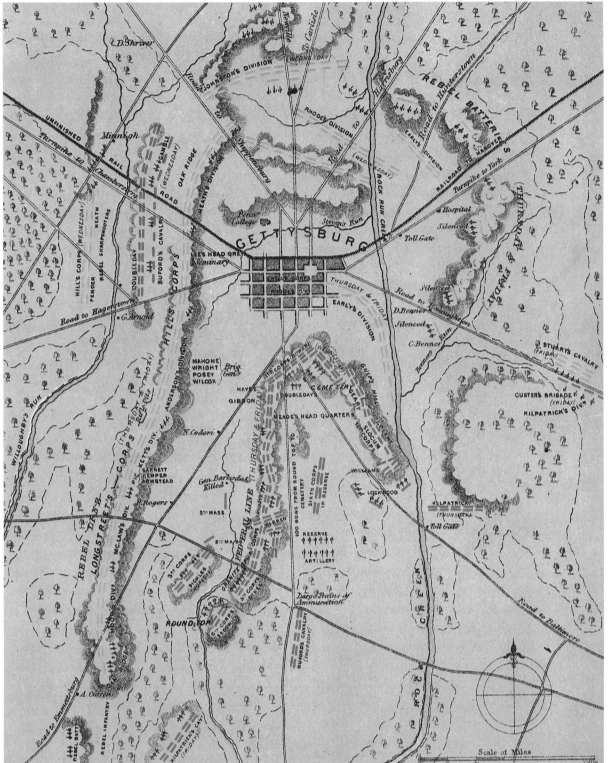

Above: Colonel John Hunt Morgan CSA (1825-64) was a fearless cavalry commander.

Left: The town of Gettysburg stood at the junction of many roads.

see his chance to get even and would seize it – to the great misfortune of the Confederacy.

By mid-June Hill had left Fredericksburg and the whole Army of Northern Virginia was on the move through Pennsylvania to the northwest, circling Washington. Lee did not yet know that Hooker and the Army of the Potomac were paralleling them to the east like a shadow, staying between the Southern army and Washington. As the opposing forces marched northwest the two cavalries, both on reconnaissance, fought a running series of skirmishes, the Yankee troopers clearly demonstrating their new confidence. Though largely indecisive,

these skirmishes served to keep the Rebel cavalry at a distance from the Federal infantry, and as a result Stuart was not at all sure where to find the bulk of the enemy.

This problem was compounded when Stuart proposed to Lee that his men repeat an old stunt of theirs – raiding completely around the Federal army. In an ambiguously-worded order, Lee seemed to approve the plan. Stuart set out on what seemed to be his great chance to revenge his humiliation at Brandy Station – though, naturally, his real duty was to raid the Union supply lines in the rear, at which game Stuart was a past master. Soon, how-

Opposite: The Confederate Army felt that they could defeat the Union easily with Lee in command.

Right: The battle began by accident when Confederate troops from Heth's division accidently came upon a Federal Cavalry division.

Opposite: General Longstreet wanted the invasion campaign to be offensive in strategy, but defensive in tactics.

Below: General Richard S Ewell commanded one of the Confederate Corps at Gettysburg.

ever, The Cavalier found he was getting out of his depth. The Federals were much more spread out than expected; to avoid them Stuart had to detour further and further east. He was finally to be out of touch with Lee for ten days and did not rejoin the army until the second night of the battle. The effect on Lee's campaign was devastating – the Confederate army had lost its eyes, was in effect marching blindfolded into enemy territory.

Thus Lee moved through Pennsylvania, his forces widely separated, not knowing that Hooker had crossed the Potomac, was squarely on the Confederate flank and on the shortest road to Richmond as well. Finally on 28 June Lee learned two important pieces of information, as staff officer Moxley Sorrel relates:

With us was a scout, more properly a spy, who was a man of about thirty ... and altogether an extraordinary character. His time seemed to be passed about equally within our lines and the enemy's. Harrison (such was his name) ... went everywhere, even through Stanton's War Office in Washington, and brought in much ...

One night ... I was aroused by the provost guard bringing up a suspicious prisoner. It was Harrison, the scout, filthy and ragged, showing some rough work and exposure. His report ... described how the enemy were even then marching in great numbers ... with the intention apparently of concentrating [nearby]. ... I woke General Longstreet, who immediately sent the scout to Lee. The general heard him with great composure and minuteness. It was on this, the report of a single scout, in the absence of [Stuart's] cavalry, that the army moved.

Artillery and infantry
were forced to fire upon
one another, inflicting
grave damage on both
sides.

Right: Brigadier General John Buford commanded the division discovered by the Confederates.

Below: The new commander of the Union forces was General George G Meade (1815-72).

Now Lee knew that the Federals were on his trail. He also heard from Harrison the interesting news that the Army of the Potomac had a new commander. Joe Hooker's humiliation at Chancellorsville had not been forgotten by Washington; they had only been waiting for the right political moment to replace him. That day came on 28 June, when Hooker was cashiered and the command given to General George G Meade over his own protests – few Union generals indeed wanted that doomed command. (Hearing the orders, Meade had only half-humorously joked, 'Well, I've been tried and condemned without a hearing, and I suppose I shall have to go to execution.') It was the fifth change of command in ten months for the Army of the Potomac, and no one knew if Meade would do any better than the others. He was a drawn and gloomy man, still suffering from a wound the previous year, and his foul temper was legendary among his subordinates. But if not truly brilliant, Meade was to prove a tough and competent opponent. Lee prophesied accurately, 'General Meade will make no blunder on my front.'

Now realizing the enemy was on his flank, Lee decided to concentrate at the nearest place handy, which happened to be Gettysburg, Pennsylvania, a little town at the crossing of many roads. Lee was by no means planning a battle there; he could not in any case, for with Stuart gone he was still not quite sure where the Army of the Potomac was. He was concentrating simply in order to discourage operations on the rear of his army. If it came to battle his intended position was to be nearby Cashtown, which would be ideal for defense.

Meade, however, had made the same decision – to concentrate at Gettysburg – and made it for the same reason: convenience. Like Lee, he was not entirely certain were his enemy was. His real goal was to settle into a defensive position at Pipe Creek, 15 miles southeast of Gettysburg.

Thus the most terrible battle ever fought on American soil was about to break out by accident. The course the battle would take was also significantly to be determined by happenstance – the Confederate army was by then fairly tightly concentrated, the Union army spread out; Jeb Stuart was still skylarking, Lee still blindfolded; and some of A P Hill's men had heard they might find some shoes in town.

On 1 July, John Buford's Federal cavalry division was scouting in Gettysburg. Buford, a tough and prematurely aged cavalry soldier who had less than a year to live, had felt a premonition they would run into trouble. Watching from a ridge just to the west of town that morning, Buford saw the trouble

BUFORD'S CAVALRY OPPOSING THE
CONFEDERATE ADVANCE UPON

coming: a column of enemy troops, preceded by skirmishers, slogging toward town. They were a brigade of Harry Heth's division of Hill's corps, and they were looking for shoes, not Yankees. The 2500 Federal troopers dismounted, formed a thin line of battle from McPherson's Ridge north to Seminary Ridge, and began firing away with their new Spencer repeating carbines. The Rebels spread out and returned fire. Over the next two hours Buford and his few men performed heroic service, holding back the oncoming enemy like a dam and preparing the way for the Union fortunes to come.

By ten in the morning Confederates were pouring in from everywhere. General William D Pender had arrived to support Heth and the Federal cavalrymen were now badly outnumbered, but still they held on. Buford had sent a plea for help to John Reynolds and I Corps. About ten o'clock in the morning Reynolds arrived just in front of his corps, expertly surveyed the situation, and rushed to position his oncoming infantry. Soon the Confederates spotted the black hats of the Union Iron Brigade, a legendary outfit since their first battle at the Second Manassas. The Federals could hear the Rebels muttering, 'Here are those damned black-hat fellers agin.' 'Tain't no militia – that's the Army of the Potomac!' Thus the Southern soldiers found out whom they were fighting.

Soldiers were falling into position in waves on both sides of the line. For a time the Union position stabilized a little. Federal general Abner Doubleday captured his old friend General James Archer and a large part of his brigade; Archer was the first of Lee's general officers ever to be captured. An observer remembered the scene:

[Archer] evidently had expected a easy 'walk over,' judging from his disappointed manner after he was captured. A guard brought him back to General Doubleday, who, in a very cordial manner, – they having been cadets at West Point

together – said: 'Good-morning Archer! How are you? I am glad to see you!' General Archer replied: 'Well. I am *not* glad to see *you*, by a dammed sight!'

Buford's cavalry dismounted to hold the ground until they were relieved.

Left: General John Reynolds, considered the best soldier in the Union Army, commanded I Corps.

Below: Reynolds was killed by a stray bullet early in the battle.

On the first day of the
battle, the Union
artillery position on
Cemetery Ridge became
a focal point of the Union
line.

Slowly the Federals were pushed back from McPherson's Ridge to Seminary Ridge, but they were not in retreat. Hundreds of Southerners were captured after vicious fighting in a railroad cut to the south. General Reynolds rode behind his lines, strengthening the position. He was considered by many to be the best soldier in the Union army, the man who should have been commander of the Army of the Potomac all along. But that did not stop the sharpshooter's bullet that knocked Reynolds dead from his saddle early in the action.

At noon there was an ominous lull. Heth formed his men south of the Cashtown road. Federal generals Doubleday and James Wadsworth dressed their lines along and in front of Seminary Ridge as the rest of the I Corps arrived and fell into line. About one in the afternoon Oliver O Howard's XI Corps, who had been routed by Jackson at Chancellorsville, began arriving. The divisions of Carl Schurz and Francis Barlow took positions to the north, on the Federal right. Howard decided to leave an artillery reserve on Cemetery Hill, just south of town.

Howard's putting the battery on Cemetery Hill turned out to be one of those decisions that win battles, for the Union was about to need that position desperately. Lee by early afternoon had

decided to throw everything he had at the Federals. Ewell, leading Jackson's old corps, descended from the North onto the Federal right. The still luckless XI Corps were flanked as they had been at Chancellorsville and finally caved in. Frantic calls went back to the two nearest Union corps. The XI Corps meanwhile fled through Gettysburg and there in the streets found no safety. One of their officers describes the flight:

The Eleventh Corps broke, followed by the entire line. As the troops hurried toward the town, the disorder increased. The First Corps retired more slowly, and as a portion of the two Corps met, the confusion was great. The Confederates poured volley after volley into the compact mass, and captured about 2500 prisoners. A sudden panic arose. Our regiment headed into an alley. Unfortunately, it offered no way out except a very narrow doorway; but the enemy had already piled a barrier of dead Union soldiers in its front, and two-thirds of the regiment was lost.

A Federal cannoneer remembered the struggle as the I Corps was pressed:

The enemy ... made his appearance in grand

The hillside known as Little Round Top was the scene of some of the bloodiest fighting of the war.

shape. His line stretched nearly a mile in length. First we could see the tips of their colorstaffs coming up over the little ridge, then the points of their bayonets, and then the Johnnies themselves, coming on with a steady tramp, tramp, and with loud yells . . . In quick, sharp tones, like successive reports of a repeating rifle, came our captain's orders: 'Load . . . Canister . . . Double! . . .'

Directly in our front the Rebel infantry had been forced to halt and lie down, by the tornado of canister that we had given them. But the regiments to their right kept on, as if to cut us off from the rest of our troops.

Then ensued probably the most desperate fight ever waged between artillery and infantry at close range without a particle of cover on either side. They gave us volley after volley in front and flank, and we gave them double canister as fast as we could load . . .

Up and down the line men were reeling and falling; splinters flying from wheels and axles where bullets hit; in the rear, horses tearing and plunging, drivers yelling, shells bursting, shot shrieking overhead, howling about our ears . . . the musketry crashing on three sides of us . . . all crash on crash

and peal on peal, smoke, dust, splinters, blood, wreck and carnage indescribable.

The Confederates pressed on relentlessly, scattering the I Corps before them. It was an all-too-

Above: Letting off steam between the battles.

The Federal position on Round Top was attacked on the second day.

The Battle of Gettysburg lasted for three days.

Above: General John Bankhead Magruder CSA (1810-71).

Right: Meade ordered his troops into position on the high ground spreading out from Cemetery Hill.

Opposite: General Winfield Scott Hancock USA commanded the Union II Corps.

familiar story for the Army of the Potomac: Lee had massed his troops to gain local superiority and was crushing his enemy piece by piece. But there remained the XI Corps artillery reserve to the south of Cemetery Hill. As evening descended, Federal general Winfield Scott Hancock arrived at that position, ordered by Meade to take charge there. From those heights Hancock saw his army apparently in confused rout all over the field. There were at most 5000 men left available out of the entire I and XI Corps. Shouting and cursing, Hancock slowly rallied the stragglers around Howard's battery on Cemetery Hill. As dark came on he had a serviceable position; in fact, maybe a very good position indeed. Noticing that Culp's Hill, just to the west, might be vulnerable, Hancock sent some troops to occupy it. Another serviceable position, maybe.

Across the way, General Ewell was taking a good look at Cemetery Ridge. After arriving in the afternoon, Lee had asked Ewell to assault that hill 'if possible.' That courteous 'if possible' would have inspired Stonewall Jackson to move mountains. But 'Baldy' Ewell was no more a Jackson than any of

The soldiers of Ewell's Corps were ordered to attack the entrenched Union positions on Culp's and Cemetery Hills.

Lee's present subordinates, and he was plagued with an odd paralysis of will in those days. He decided not to try to take Cemetery Hill; the enemy artillery position looked too formidable on those heights. If Ewell had tried, American history might have been very different. That position, so vulnerable at that moment, was to become the foundation of the Union line.

Nonetheless, the South had clearly won the day on the first of July. It had pushed the enemy back and inflicted a terrible toll. A confident Lee made plans for an all-out attack as early as possible next morning. His men would walk right over the Northerners, just as so many times before. And yet things were, once again, not so good as they seemed for the South. Lee had been drawn into battle at a time and on ground not of his own choosing; dictating the time and place to fight had constituted much of his advantage in previous victories – and was what he had lacked at Antietam. With Stuart still away, Lee did not know exactly where Meade's forces were; to the conclusion of the battle he believed Meade did not have his whole force in position. Jackson was gone, and Longstreet recal-

citrant. The enemy was in its own territory, fighting for its own soil. And though the Union army had been forced back, they had been driven onto positions that were stronger than anyone, North or South, seemed to realize that night – except perhaps for Hancock, who surveyed the area with increasing satisfaction.

This time there were to be no uncommitted corps in the Union army, as there had been at Antietam and Chancellorsville. Meade was cautious, too cautious in the long run, but this time he was going to give it everything he had. All night and next morning he moved troops into position on high ground, the lines spreading out from Cemetery Hill in a fishhook pattern on the heights, the northern end curling around to Culp's Hill. Good as his ground was, however, Meade's concern for the right flank – he feared the enemy could get around it to his rear – led him to build up the right and stint the left flank, especially the two Round Tops to the south, which thus became his weak point.

And it was squarely on that left flank that Lee was planning to strike on the second day of battle. Once again, Longstreet demurred – it seemed to him impossible to assault the enemy on those heights. Instead, he proposed a strategic envelopment, moving around behind the Federals. Longstreet wrote of his struggle to persuade Lee of this strategy, on the first night of the battle:

I found [General Lee] on the summit of Seminary Ridge watching the enemy concentrate on the opposite hill. He pointed out their position to me. I took my glasses and made as careful a survey as I could from that point. After five or ten minutes I turned to General Lee and said:

'If we could have chosen a point to meet our plans of operation, I do not think we could have found a better one than that upon which they are now concentrating. All we have to do is to throw our army around by their left, get a strong position and wait, and if they fail to attack us we shall have everything in condition to move back tomorrow night in the direction of Washington, selecting beforehand a good position into which we can place our troops to receive battle next day. Finding our object is Washington or that army, the Federals will be sure to attack us. When they attack, we shall beat them, as we proposed to do before we left Fredericksburg . . .'

'No,' said General Lee; 'the enemy is there, and I am going to attack him there.'

I suggested that such a move as I proposed would give us control of the roads leading to Washington and Baltimore, and reminded General Lee of our original plans [of being offensive in strategy and defensive in tactics]. If we had fallen behind Meade and had insisted on staying between him and Washington, he would have been compelled to attack and would have been badly beaten. General Lee answered, 'No; they are there in position, and I am going to whip them or they are going to whip me.'

Lee ordered an attack early next morning on the Union left, around the Round Tops. If he could overrun these positions he would roll up the Federal line like a rug. The Confederate army was then stretched around the fishhook-shape of Meade's lines, Ewell on the left with the divisions of Johnson, Early, and Rodes; Hill was in the center with Pender and Anderson's divisions (Heth's in reserve): Longstreet was on the left, leading the attack with Hood and McLaws. The attack was to sweep obliquely from the Southern right to left: Ewell was instructed to begin a strong diversion on the left when he heard Longstreet's guns.

It was a workable enough plan, but on 2 July it was bungled by nearly everybody – though there was enough of a blunder on the Union side that Lee's plan had a good chance of working. To begin with, Ewell balked at attacking entrenched Union positions on Culp's and Cemetery Hills; he made only a few ineffectual efforts during the day, far less than the major diversion intended. Besides, Ewell never got his signal from the right during the morning. Longstreet, supposed to attack the Union left at dawn, delayed through the morning and into the afternoon, saying he was waiting for Pickett's fresh division, which had not yet arrived. So Longstreet was reluctant, Ewell waffling, and Jackson sorely missed indeed.

But Longstreet's delay finally gave the Federals

Above: General Jubal Anderson Early CSA (1816-94)

Left: Longstreet's Corps attacked the Union left.

enough rope nearly to hang themselves. The blunder was accomplished by Union general Daniel E Sickles, who repeated his mistake at Chancellorsville by moving out of position. Sickles had been ordered to occupy the Round Tops, and thus firmly anchor the Federal left. Instead, he decided on his own that the ground occupied by his II Corps along the southern part of Cemetery Ridge was not high enough; besides, there were Rebels out there moving toward his left (they were Longstreet's and John B Hood's men). Itching for a fight, Sickles moved his corps forward without orders to slightly

The Confederate snipers
in Devil's Den aided the
attack on Little Round
Top.

Above: General Joseph O Shelby CSA.

higher ground on a line from the Peach Orchard through the Wheat Field to Devil's Den, at the foot of Little Round Top. About four o'clock in the afternoon an enraged Meade rode over and ordered Sickles to pull this precarious salient back. As they argued, an earsplitting cannonade erupted square on Sickle's left flank – 46 of Longstreet's guns. Meade curtly observed that it was too late to pull back now; the III Corps would have to fight it out as best they could. Meade then galloped back to forestall the inevitable disaster – as best he could.

Watching from the height, Union lieutenant Franklin A Haskell – who left remarkable eye-witness account, written directly after the battle – saw the result:

Upon the front and right flank of Sickles came sweeping the infantry of Longstreet and Hill. Hitherto there had been skirmishing and artillery practice – now the battle begins; for amid the heavier smokes and longer tongues of flame of the batteries, now began to appear the countless flashes, and the long, fiery sheet of the muskets, and rattle of the volleys mingled with the thunder of the guns. We see the long gray lines [Hood and Lafayette McLaws' divisions] come sweeping down upon Sickles' front, and mix with the battle smoke; now the same colors emerge from the bushes and orchards upon his right, and envelop his flank in the confusion of the conflict. Oh, the din and the roar, and these thirty thousand rebel wolf-cries! What a hell is there down that valley!

By six o'clock Sickles had been carried from the field minus a leg and General David B Birney had taken command, his left already giving way. It was around that time when both sides suddenly seemed to recognize the critical importance of the Round Tops. What ensued was a desperate race by both armies to occupy those positions, which were the key to the Union line – if the Confederates could take them, they would be in position to move up the ridge and roll up Meade's line, just as Lee had intended.

However, yet another disagreement developed in the Confederate command. Hood insisted, quite rightly, that he should attack from the south, outflanking the poorly defended left of the Union line. Longstreet may well have agreed with Hood, but Lee had firmly ordered an assault onto Little Round Top. To Hood's several entreaties, Long-street stolidly replied, 'General Lee's orders are to attack up the Emmittsburg road [onto Little Round Top].' Perhaps Longstreet was simply tired of trying to change Lee's mind. Convinced it would not work, Hood finally followed the orders and led his troops toward Little Round Top. Soon Hood was wounded and carried from the field, but his attack came within a hair's breadth of succeeding.

Sometimes the fate of great battles and of great nations concentrate on the actions of a very few men over a very few minutes. One of these men, for a few

Below: Colonel Joshua Lawrence Chamberlain USA, later President of Bowdoir College.

critical moments, was Federal General Gouverneur K Warren, who arrived at Little Round Top as Hood's men were climbing the little boulder-studded knoll. To his dismay, Warren saw that this place was the linchpin of the Union position and that there were no troops on it at all, only a signal station. He sent an imperative note to Meade and awaited results while watching 500 men of the 15th Alabama climbing toward him with shouts of victory.

As bullets began to play around Warren, a few Federal cannons arrived and began sending canister into the enemy, slowing them. Then at a run came 350 men of the 20th Maine commanded by young Colonel Joshua Chamberlain, who just one year before had left his position as professor at Bowdoin College to realize his dream of becoming a soldier. Now it was up to Chamberlain and the men of Maine to save or to lose the Army of the Potomac. William Oates, colonel of the 15th Alabama, narrates what ensued as he led the charge on the 20th Maine:

I again ordered the advance, and knowing the officers and men of that gallant old regiment, I felt sure that they would follow their commander anywhere in the line of duty. I passed through the line waving my sword, shouting, 'Forward, men, to the ledge!' and was promply followed by the command in splendid style. We drove the Federals from their strong defensive position; five times they rallied and charged us, twice coming so near that some of my men had to use the bayonet, but in vain was their effort. It was our time now to deal death and destruction to a gallant foe, and the account was speedily settled. I led this charge and sprang upon the ledge of rock, using my pistol within musket length, when the rush of my men drove the Maine men from the ledge along the line ... The Twentieth Maine was driven back from this ledge, but not farther than to the next ledge on the mountain-side ...

There never were harder fighters than the Twentieth Maine men and their gallant Colonel. His skill and persistency and the great bravery of his men saved Little Round Top and the Army of the Potomac from defeat.

Unable to penetrate Chamberlain's line, the Alabamians crumbled and ran back down Little Round Top. Their confusion was such that one Confederate officer was seen with one hand offering his sword in surrender while firing his pistol with the other. Heading for cover behind a stone wall below, the fleeing Southerners ran head-on into the rifles of the 20th Maine's skirmishers, who had been pre-sumed killed. Other Federal units began arriving on the hilltop, among them the 140th New York. Coming up over Little Round Top at a dead run with unloaded guns and no bayonets, the New Yorkers simply charged straight at the enemy, their bodies their only weapons. Somehow this bizarre counterattack worked; the surprised Confederates pulled back, Little Round Top, and thus the anchor of the Union line, was safe; Federal soldiers began piling in to reinforce it.

But no one could save the rest of the devastated III Corps. Surrounded on three sides, Sickles' salient caved in, and McLaws made for the gap that opened up between the fleeing III Corps and Hancock's II Corps. From all over his line, Hancock, ordered by Meade to stop the rout, feverishly rushed troops to plug the gap. Again the battle came down to a few men, this time Union artillerymen around Trostle's Farm. There just after seven o'clock artillery captain John Bigelow held back William Barksdale's Mississippians long enough for a stronger battery to be mounted to the rear. Fighting surged into the artillery positions, the cannoneers beating back the Rebels with rammers and handspikes and fists; men rolled on the ground slugging away like barroom rowdies. At length Barksdale was killed and his men could not get through the gap.

It had been a day of almosts for the Confederacy, but Lee was by no means finished. Southern efforts were shifting steadily northward; the next blow came in the Federal center, on Cemetery Ridge. Hancock, commanding that part of the field, saw a flag moving toward him, apparently from his own lines. He asked angrily what his men were retreating for; a volley showed him that it was a Rebel column, some 50 yards away. Hancock rode back and found

Colonel Colville of the 1st Minnesota. 'Do you see those colours?', Hancock demanded. Colville did. 'Well, capture them!', roared Hancock. Still in marching column, the 1st Minnesota charged the Confederates, who fell back and then rallied, getting the Federals into a pocket. The Minnesotans' line held on somehow, and when the Confederates finally fell back the 1st Minnesota had 47 men left of the 262 who had so gallantly charged – 82 percent casualties, the worst of the war.

So Southern attacks on the left and center of the Federal line had failed, each seemingly by a hair's breadth, each saved for the Union at the last minute: the Union command under Meade had finally learned to maneuver their troops to best advantage on the battlefield, just as Lee and his staff had always done. And the Army of the Potomac had fought as well as anyone could have asked. As the fighting began to die down on the center and left, the Confederates settled into position at the base of the Round Tops, in Devil's Den, and along the base of Cemetery Ridge.

About six in the evening there had been a threat to the Federal right. After an artillery barrage Ewell finally made a move on Culp's Hill, held by Howard's XI Corps. Federal strength there was depleted due to troops being sent south. Edward Johnson's brigade, on the Confederate right, advanced up the hill toward strong but sparsely-manned Union breastworks. Once again Federal

Meade ordered Hancock to take charge of the troops on Cemetery Hill.

Above: The culmination of the three-day battle arrived with the charge of Longstreet's Corps, which is better known as Pickett's charge.

Below: General Nathan Bedford Forrest CSA (1821-77).

reinforcements arrived in time to stop the attack, and after eight o'clock Johnson's men settled into position on the slopes.

An hour later, in the last fighting of 2 July, Jubal Early's Confederates made it into XI Corps batteries on Cemetery Hill. For the second time that day Union cannoneers and Rebel infantry fought hand-to-hand, the Dutchmen swearing vigorously in German. After an hour of bitter fighting Early called it quits when Federal reinforcements arrived for a countercharge. Except for a few confused attempts on Culp's hill by Ewell's men during the night, the second day's fighting was finally done.

The day had been a draw at best. Still, for the Confederate survivors that night there was the strange and profound joy of soldiers after battle – the joy of having come alive through the other side of hell, and the comradeship amounting almost to love for those who shared that journey at one's side. The idea that they might be defeated had apparently not occurred to the Army of Northern Virginia; they were unaccustomed to the idea. They were certain that Lee would know what to do to finish off the Yankees tomorrow.

As dawn broke on 3 July, the Union army looked out from the heights and waited. Over on the right, at Culp's Hill, there was soon some inconclusive action. Ewell opened up a cannonade and then sent his men up the hill. The Federals, in good log-reinforced trenches, turned back the attack easily. About ten-thirty a deep silence spread once again over the battlefield, and again the Union army waited, resting on their arms in the oppressive heat

of approaching noon. Some opined that the Rebels were about to retreat.

But once again, things were not as they appeared in the Army of Northern Virginia. That morning was a time of the most intense preparation within Southern lines, and also of the last confrontation between Lee and Longstreet. For the last time Longstreet struggled to convince his commander of the necessity for a defensive strategy, to try an envelopment, this time around the Union right. In reply Lee pointed imperiously with his fist to Cemetery Hill, saying, 'The enemy is there, and I am going to strike him.'

The whole army was to go into action together, Ewell to start with a fullscale assault on Culp's Hill (which came to nothing), Stuart to go around the Union right and strike their supply line, E P Alexander to mount a massive artillery barrage on the Federal center, A P Hill to support Longstreet, and Longstreet himself to organize a direct assault into the heart of the Union position on Cemetery Ridge: for the last time in the war, it was to be a grand charge in the old Napoleonic style.

Greatly agitated, Longstreet expostulated, 'General, I have been a soldier all my life. It is my opinion that no 15,000 men ever arrayed can take that position.' Lee, calm as always, proceeded to give his orders. Unusually, for Lee, all of them were fantasies; not one part of them had a reasonable chance of success. And to guide these fantasies Lee depended on Longstreet, his old war horse. That was perhaps the most utterly fantastic part of it all. But in placing absolute faith in a trusted subordinate, Lee the man was entirely in character.

Longstreet was an old soldier, and so he carried out the orders, orders whose outcome he knew only to well. That morning was his Gethsamane. The artillery was positioned and the barrage executed, the Confederate guns exhausting most of their ammunition. It was the most terrible barrage of cannonfire ever heard on the American continent, perhaps the worst in history: 172 guns on the Confederate side, 80 answering on the Union side. The discharges blended into one continuous and apocalyptic roar that seemed to shake the very earth to its foundations. A Union observer described the effect in Union lines:

Right, left and rear of us, caissons exploded, scudding fragments of wheels, woodwork, shell, and shot one hundred feet into the air, like the eruption of a volcano . . . For an hour and a half crash followed crash. Some of the shot shrieked and hissed, some whistled; some came with muffled growl; some with howls like rushing, circling winds. Some spat and sputtered; others uttered unearthly groans or hoarsely howled their mission to death. Holes like graves were gouged in the earth by exploding shells . . .

If a constellation of meteoric worlds had exploded above our heads, it would have scarcely been more terrible than this iron rain of death furiously hurled upon us. Over all these sounds were heard the shrieks and groans of the wounded and dying.

While the cannons were firing, Longstreet arranged the lines for the charge. In front were two divisions, J Johnston Pettigrew on the left and the fresh troops of George E Pickett on the right. To the middle rear was the division of Isaac R Trimble (this placement was a mistake, for Trimble was supposed to be in echelon to the left, supporting the flank where fire would be heaviest). Hill and Ewell had been ordered to support the charge, but in the end they did practically nothing.

For some reason history decided to call this action 'Pickett's Charge,' though Longstreet was actually in command. But General George Pickett was certainly one of the most enthusiastic soldiers on the field. A perfumed and ringletted dandy, Pickett had been last in his class at West Point, and indeed would likely not have gotten in at all without the influence of his good friend Abraham Lincoln – whose name Pickett would not allow to be slandered in his presence.

But Pickett was a dashing soldier, and he had a sweetheart, a girl of nineteen whom he loved utterly

General Meade's Headquarters was shelled by the Confederate Artillery.

and wrote daily. On this day Pickett wrote to her twice, once before and once after the charge. Minutes before his division moved out, he wrote:

Our line of battle faces Cemetery Ridge. The men are lying in the rear, and the hot July sun pours its scorching rays almost vertically down on them. The suffering is almost unbearable.

I have never seen Old Peter [meaning Longstreet] so grave and troubled. For several minutes after I had saluted him he looked at me without speaking. Then in an agonized voice, the reserve all gone, he said, 'Pickett, I am being crucified. I have instructed Alexander to give you your orders, for I can't.'

While he was yet speaking, a note was brought to me from Alexander. After reading it I handed it to Peter, asking if I should obey and go forward. He looked at me for a moment, then held out his hand . . . I shall never forget the look in his face nor the clasp of his hand, and I saw tears glistening on his cheeks and beard. The stern old war horse, God bless him, was weeping for his men and, I know, praying too that this cup might pass from them. It is almost three o'clock.

YOUR SOLDIER

So Longstreet the old soldier, who had seen everything there was to see in battle, was weeping for his men as they strode out. On Cemetery Ridge the men of the Union II Corps rose to their feet from behind a low stone wall, seeing something that took their breath away: fifteen thousand of their enemy dressed immaculately in a front a half-mile wide and three ranks deep, colors flying, sunlight flashing on musket barrels and drawn swords, officers galloping up and down, the men's steps firm and determined and irresistible. Silently, the soldiers of the Union watched their enemy approach, and it was a terrible and magnificent thing to behold.

Then the defenders returned to business – guns loaded and cocked, thumbs checking the percussion caps, cartridges lined up to hand on the ground. With a running rattle thousands of muskets stretched out over the stone wall. Lieutenant Alonzo Cushing of Battery 4A, wounded three times in the Rebel cannonade, was being propped up by a sergeant amidst the wreckage of his battery; his two remaining guns awaited his orders. Terrible as the cannonade had been, the Confederate gunners had been consistently firing too high; most of the fury had fallen behind the ridge rather than on the front line, where it was most needed. The Union soldiers in front were ready to receive the foe; the Union artillery had been careful to conserve its ammunition.

Opposite: General George Edward Pickett CSA (1825-75) commanded the division of Longstreet's Corps that charged Cemetery Ridge.

Following spread: Confederate dead after the Battle of Gettysburg.

Below: One of the Federal Artillery Batteries that repulsed Pickett's Charge.

Above: Cadets from the Virginia Military Institute fought at the Battle of New Market.

The Confederate lines marched across half a mile of open fields, the grain parting gently before them; they moved over the plank fences of the Emmitsburg road, closing in toward the little clump of trees at the angle of the stone wall on Cemetery Ridge. The Federal artillery watched, poised.

Then a storm of shell opened on the Rebels. Holes appeared in their lines, colors fell and were retrieved. Still the men marched steadily forward. Now they came into shrapnel range, now into canister range. Southerners fell in tens, in dozens, in hundreds; great gaps were torn in the lines. Across the way the Rebel batteries had few shells to fire in reply. The Confederate right flank brushed past some concealed Vermont regiments, who opened up a blistering musket fire.

A hundred yards away now. Soon the left side of the Federal line was firing; the Confederates on that flank begin drifting to their left, toward an angle in the stone wall near the little clump of trees. The 8th Ohio, posted forward as skirmishers, began to enfilade Pettigrew's column on the Confederate left. One of that regiment recalled the sight:

The front of the column was nearly up the slope, and within a few yards of the line of the Second Corps' front and its batteries, when suddenly a terrific fire from every available gun from the Cemetery to Round Top Mountain burst upon them. The distinct, graceful lines of the rebels underwent an instantaneous transformation. They were at once enveloped in a dense cloud of smoke and dust. Arms, heads, blankets, guns, and knapsacks were thrown and tossed into the clear air. Their attack, as they advanced, was strewn with dead and wounded. A moan went up from the field, distinctly to be heard amid the storm of battle; but on they went, too much enveloped in smoke and dust now to permit us to distinguish their lines or movements, for the mass appeared more like a cloud of moving smoke and dust than a column of troops.

Both Rebel flanks began to falter, then the left gave way. But the center moved forward still, like a spearhead. Pettigrew was down, Generals Garnett and Kemper of Pickett's corps were mortally wounded. Union artilleryman Alonzo Cushing had one gun left; he ordered it wheeled down to the stone wall to fire point-blank with triple-shotted canister into the oncoming mass of Rebels. He fired his last charge just as a bullet found him and he fell dead. The spearhead was at the wall now, and some had leaped over it. They were led by General Lewis Armistead, holding his hat on his sword to show his men the way. Armistead was headed for a strange rendezvous with one of his oldest and dearest friends, Union general Winfield Scott Hancock.

This was it now, the high tide of the Confederacy. Armistead and a handful of men were over the stone wall, the Confederate colors were arriving one after another; Southerners were among Cushing's

wrecked battery; one of the guns was grasped by Armistead. Gibbon and Hancock were wounded, and Pennsylvanians were retreating from the over-run angle near the clump of trees. All was smoke and fire and indecipherable chaos on the open brow of the ridge.

Things happened fast now. The Pennsylvanians rallied and surged forward, Lieutenant Franklin Haskell whipping the recalcitrant with his sword. Reinforcements came from somewhere. A leaderless mob of Federals swarmed around the enemy spearhead while cannons continued tearing apart the Rebels in front. Armistead was down, gasping out his life. Two accounts recall this moment, the peak of the battle and the peak of the entire war:

The men in gray were doing all that was possible to keep off the mixed bodies of men who were moving upon them swiftly and without hesitation, keeping up so close and continuous a fire that at last its effects became terrible. I could feel the touch of the men to my right and left, as we neared the edge of the copse. The grove was fairly jammed with Pickett's men, in all positions, lying and kneeling. Back from the edge were many standing and firing over those in front. By the side of several who were firing . . . were others with their hands up, in token of surrender. In particular I noticed two men, not a musket-length away, one aiming so that I could look into his musket-barrel; the other, lying on his back, coolly ramming home a cartridge.

The jostling, swaying lines on either side boil and roar and dash their foamy spray, two hostile billows of a fiery ocean. Thick flashes stream from the wall; thick volleys answer from the crest. No threats or expostulation now; only example and encouragement. All depths of passion are stirred, and all combative fire, down to their deep foundations. Individuality is drowned in a sea of clamor; and timid men, breathing the breath of the multitude, are brave. The frequent dead and wounded lie where they stagger and fall; there is no humanity for them now, and none can be spared to care for them. The men do not cheer, or shout – they growl; and over that uneasy sea, heard with the roar of musketry, sweeps the muttered thunder of a storm of growls.

All at once, it was finished. The Confederate spearhead seemed to dissolve. Some Southerners fell back; others threw down their muskets, raising their hands in surrender. The Confederacy had reached its highwater mark, had receded, and the crest of Cemetery Ridge was won for the Union. The irresistable charge of a few minutes before became a rabble of survivors pouring back down the slope.

Meade rode up from the rear, his face very white, and inquired of Lieutenant Haskell, 'How is it going here?' 'I believe, General, the enemy is repulsed,' Haskell replied. 'Thank God,' Meade said, and added a choked cheer.

Opposite: The South lost over a third of the 75,000 men engaged in the battle. The lucky ones were captured.

Meade and his staff at Culpeper, Virginia, two months after the Battle of Gettysburg.

Above: In November, part of the battlefield was dedicated as a memorial to the fallen Union troops.

Opposite: U S Grant took the city of Vicksburg, thus opening the Mississippi River, the same day that the Battle of Gettysburg ended.

Below: Lieutenant General John Clifford Pemberton CSA (1814-81) surrendered the city of Vicksburg.

Lying on a stretcher dictating orders, the wounded Hancock was interrupted by an aide, who handed him a watch and a few personal effects. They were from Armistead; his last words were a message to his old friend: 'Tell Hancock I have done him and my country a great injustice which I shall never cease to regret.' But all regrets had ceased for Armistead.

It was over. Strewn with thousands of dead and wounded, the battleground looked, as one soldier remarked, like 'a square mile of Tophet.' Across the way the beaten Confederates sank exhausted into their lines, rallied by Lee, who rode about saying whatever can be said after such a day. Lee also said, and meant it, 'All this had been my fault.' Even Stuart, finally arriving the previous night, had been repulsed today by Federal cavalry on the north flank. For the Army of Northern Virginia it was finally complete and unmitigated defeat that third of July. A prostrated Pickett wrote again to his sweetheart:

My brave boys were so full of hope and confident of victory as I led them forth! . . .

Well, it is all over now. The awful rain of shot and shell was a sob – a gasp . . .

Oh, how faithfully they followed me on – on – to their death, and I led them on – on – on – Oh, God!

But there was yet work to be done. Next day the Confederates formed their lines and waited for the counterattack that never came – the Army of the Potomac was too hurt and exhausted for that. In the afternoon of 4 July a downpour began, washing the blood from the grass. Lee buried his dead and withdrew. The long dismal wagon train of wounded headed back to Virginia.

The evening after the battle, General John D Imboden had encountered General Lee:

The moon shone full upon his massive features and revealed an expression of sadness that I have never before seen upon his face. Awed by his appearance I waited for him to speak until the silence became embarrassing . . .

'General, this has been a hard day on you.'

He looked up, and replied mournfully:

'Yes, it has been a sad, sad day to us,' and immediately relapsed into his thoughtful mood and attitude . . . After perhaps a minute or two, he suddenly straightened up to his full height, and turning to me with more animation and excitement of manner than I had ever seen in him before, for he was a man of wonderful equanimity, he said in a voice tremulous with emotion:

'I never saw troops behave more magnificently than Pickett's division of Virginians did today in that grand charge upon the enemy. And if they had been supported as they were to have been, – but, for some reason not yet fully explained to me, were not, – we would have held the position and the day would have been ours.' After a moment's pause he added in a loud voice, in a tone almost of agony, 'Too bad! *Too bad!* OH! TOO BAD!'

The casualties had been the worst of the war: of 88,289 Federals engaged, there were 3155 killed, 14,529 wounded, and 5365 missing, a total of 23,049 casualties. For the South, of 75,000 engaged, there were 3903 killed, 18,735 wounded, 5425 missing, a total of 28,063. Lee had lost over a third of his army.

Reaching the Potomac, the Confederates found the waters swollen and halted on the banks to wait. Meade and his army pursued cautiously, paused before the entrenched enemy, and did not attack. Lee's army withdrew across the receding Potomac the night of 13-14 July. Next day there was a rearguard skirmish at Falling Waters, in which Heth lost 500 captured and Pettigrew was killed.

Now Lee had no choice but to do what Longstreet had begged him to do at the outset – go on the defensive. But first he submitted his resignation to President Davis, assuming full responsibility for the defeat. Although he had not been served well by his generals at Gettysburg, he would not shift the blame. Davis refused the resignation, knowing that if the South had any hopes at all now, they were in Lee's hands. And Lee would prove to be a genius of defense as he had been a genius of offense.

The high tide of the Confederacy had receded in the Eastern Theater. In Mississippi, on the same day Gettysburg was lost to the South, Vicksburg fell to the army of U S Grant. Only a miracle could save the Confederacy now, and the South was running low on miracles.

CHAPTER IX

CHICKAMAUGA

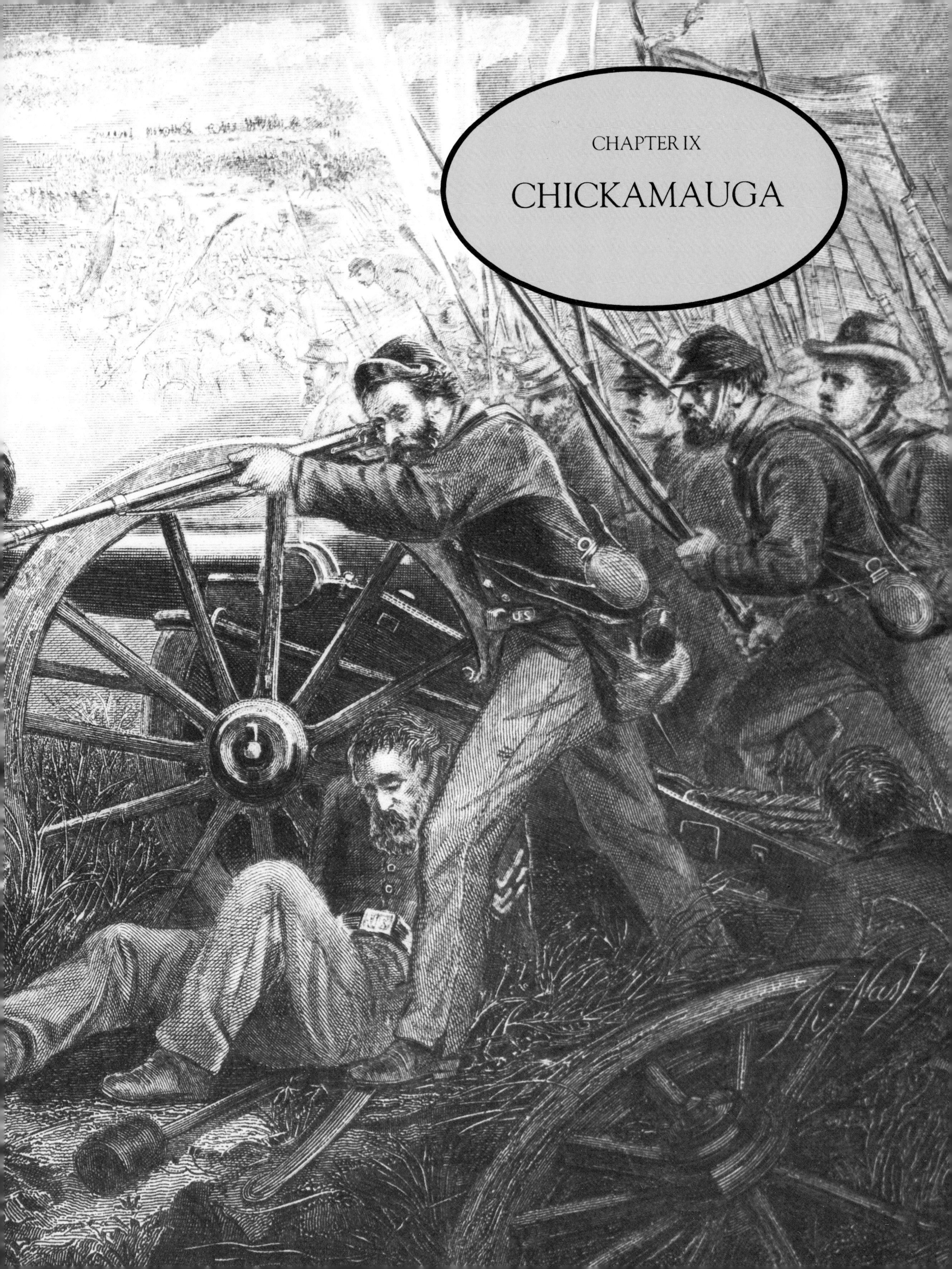

Previous spread: Federal Artillery made a stand before the attacking Confederates at Chickamauga.

Right: General Braxton Bragg CSA (1817-76) commanded the Army of Tennessee.

Below: The fortifications of Vicksburg kept the Union troops out for seven months.

Before Gettysburg, Robert E Lee had kept the hopes of the Confederacy alive with a string of glorious victories in the Eastern Theater of the war. In the Western Theater, however, things had never gone so well. Indeed, the South was defeated at every important turn deep in its own territory, most of that due to a tight-lipped, hard-fighting Union general named Ulysses S Grant. In a string of brilliant victories rivalling Lee's, Grant had risen from utter obscurity to fame with his operations at Shiloh, Forts Henry and Donelson, and in a year-long campaign of extraordinary boldness and innovation around the vital Mississippi River city of Vicksburg, which fell to the Union the same day as Gettysburg concluded – 3 July 1863.

Those two Northern victories, Gettysburg and Vicksburg, were the decisive ones of the conflict, when the fortunes of war turned the corner that would lead inexorably to victory for the North. Ironically, the decisive year of 1863 was ushered in by the indecisive battle of Stone's River, near Murfreesboro, Tennessee. There, in three days of fighting between the Federal Army of the Cumberland and the Confederate Army of Tennessee, 20,000 men fell to no advantage to either side. For nearly six months thereafter those two armies sat some 40 miles apart, waiting for their next confrontation.

Commanding the Southern forces was General Braxton Bragg, a veteran of the Mexican War and a trusted friend of President Jefferson Davis. That friendship was not to bode well for the Confederacy. Bragg was an intelligent man but a poor leader, a great maker of plans who could not bring them to fruition. Harsh, argumentative and inflexible, he was not liked by his subordinates and was served by them badly (no doubt partly because they knew he would be quick to make them scapegoats for his own mistakes). Moreover, Bragg was afflicted by severe migraine headaches and was often leading his troops in battle when both he and they would have been better off had he been home in bed.

Bragg's Federal counterpart, General William S Rosecrans, had earned his command by demonstrating a considerable talent for strategy. Early in the war Rosecrans had driven the Confederates from West Virginia, and later had been of great service to Grant in Mississippi. Rosecrans was meticulous in planning campaigns down to the last wagonwheel; he was also maddeningly slow to move. After the standoff at Stone's River, the obvious goal of his Army of the Cumberland was the last remaining truly vital city of the Confederacy – Chattanooga.

The city lay in the southeastern corner of Tennessee near the corners of Alabama and Georgia, on the banks of the Tennessee River. Railroads converged on it from all over the South. For the Confederacy, Chattanooga was the best base for operations in Tennessee and Kentucky; for the North, it was the gateway to Atlanta and all of Georgia. For these reasons, Chattanooga was the real strategic center of the Confederacy. If it were to be conquered by the Union, much of the Southern war effort would be hamstrung.

In the first six months of 1863 Bragg's Confederate Army of Tennessee lay in Tullahoma, on the road between Rosecrans' army (near Murfreesboro) and Chattanooga. In May, the Federal high command began to pressure Rosecrans to move against Bragg; this would not only threaten Chattanooga but would keep Bragg from sending men to reinforce Vicksburg, which was now besieged by Grant. Rosecrans waffled and Bragg did send some troops to Mississippi.

In mid-June Rosecrans finally got his army

moving and at once demonstrated his strategic skills. He threatened the Rebel left flank with cavalry, and when Bragg attempted to meet this threat he discovered that two Union corps, those of George H Thomas and Thomas L Crittenden, had gotten behind the Confederate right. Confused and helpless, Bragg was forced after 30 June to pull back to his nearest stronghold – Chattanooga.

Rosecrans had made a brilliant tactical move, but then he stopped again, asking for reinforcements. These were soon available, after the fall of Vicksburg in early July. But then Washington decided to occupy conquered territory rather than reinforce Rosecrans. Meanwhile, Bragg was heavily reinforced, most notably in mid-July by General Daniel H Hill, formerly of Lee's army. Also on the way were two divisions under Longstreet, which were now available after Gettysburg. (Longstreet had

suggested a move much like this well before Gettysburg).

On 5 August Rosecrans was imperatively ordered to move against Bragg. Now he faced the problem of getting the Confederates out of heavily-fortified Chattanooga. Bragg had reorganized his army to defend the city – there were two divisions each under Leonidas Polk, D H Hill, Simon B Buckner and W H T Walker, with cavalry under Joseph Wheeler and the brilliant Nathan Bedford Forrest (though Forrest only worked well in independent commands).

Rosecrans tried another strategic dodge and it worked handsomely, abetted by Bragg's poor intelligence-gathering: Federal columns appeared along the Tennessee River at several widely-spaced points; as Bragg hesitated, worrying about his supply line to the rear, the Federal army crossed the river un-

Above: General William Starkie Rosecrans USA (1819-98) became a hero after the battle of Stone's River.

Right: General Leonidas Lafayette Polk CSA (1806-64) had been a bishop in the Protestant Episcopal Church before the war.

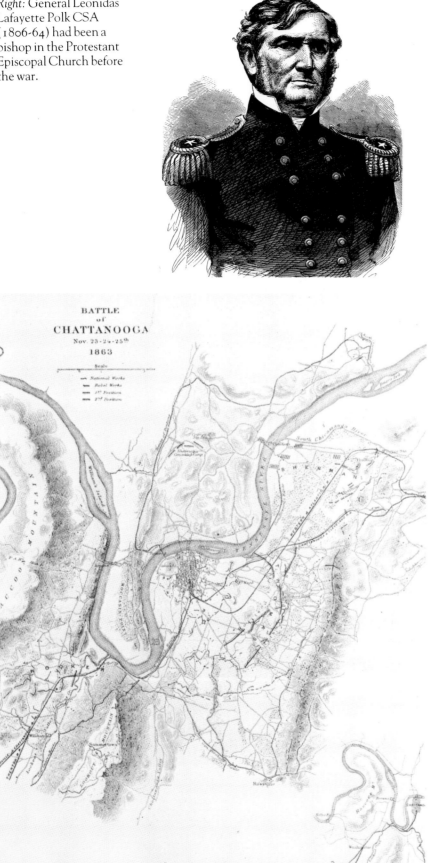

Above: The Chickamauga Rivers flowed into the Tennessee above the town of Chattanooga.

out of town with his army while the getting was good. Certain that they had the enemy on the run, the Federals made haste to pursue them into Georgia. Rosecrans boasted he would chase the Rebels to Atlanta, if not clear to the sea.

But in fact, Rosecrans was recklessly marching his army into a trap. Bragg was not fleeing; instead, he was concentrating his forces near Lafayette, Georgia, and preparing to turn and destroy the Federal army. Whether Bragg had actually planned the trap in advance is debatable. D H Hill later wrote about Bragg at that time, 'The truth is, General Bragg was bewildered by "the popping out of the rats from so many holes." The wide dispersion of the Federal forces, and their confronting him at so many points, perplexed him, instead of being a source of congratulation that such grand opportunities were offered for crushing them one by one.'

The wide dispersion Hill mentions refers to Rosecran's deployments as he moved into Georgia – the three Union corps were spread out over 50 miles of rugged country, moving through three narrow gaps in the long ridge called Lookout Mountain. Bragg had merely to bring his superior numbers to bear and crush them in detail, one corps at a time. The Federal army was ripe for the picking.

Deliberate trap or not, Bragg and his generals proceeded to spring it ineptly. The forces of General Leonidas Polk were ordered to attack Thomas on 10 September. Though Polk's men appeared in Thomas's path, nothing happened. Another attack failed to be mounted on the 11th. Two days later Bragg arrived at Chickamauga Creek, expecting Polk to have annihilated Crittenden's corps there. Polk had not budged. D H Hill would later compare Bragg's methods to Jackon's:

> Whenever a great battle is to be fought, the commander must be on the field to see that his orders are executed and to take advantage of the ever-changing phases of the conflict. Jackson leading a cavalry fight by night near Front Royal ..., Jackson at the head of the column following McClellan ... present a contrast to Bragg sending from a distance of ten miles, four consecutive orders [to Polk] for an attack at daylight, which he was never to witness.

The continuing presence of parties of Confederates in his front, all of whom seemed to be withdrawing toward Lafayette, finally tipped off Rosecrans that he was in serious trouble. On 12 September he urgently ordered his wings to converge toward the center and concentrate on the west side of Chickamauga Creek, near Lafayette. Bragg, meanwhile, was also concentrating his forces near the creek and was impatiently awaiting the arrival of Longstreet's divisions. When they arrived Bragg would have over 65,000 men to Rosecrans' less than 60,000.

Rosecrans had divined what Bragg's strategy would be in the battle, which was to move around

opposed west of the city and Crittenden marched on Chattanooga.

Confronted by an enemy seeming to appear all over the map, Bragg evacuated Chattanooga on 6 September and headed south into Georgia. It was actually a wise move on Bragg's part – he was getting the Union left and cut off their line of retreat – a road to Chattanooga. The Federal commander thus paid special attention to his left, placing General George H Thomas in command there. Whether or not this was fortuitous, the positioning of the indomitable Thomas was to prove a decision most fortunate indeed for the fate of the Union army. (Years before, Thomas had been a member of Bragg's artillery battery in the Mexican War – the two other officers in the battery being D H Hill and, later Union officer, John Reynolds, killed at Gettysburg. Bragg to this day spoke fondly of Thomas.)

Rosecrans' deployment was not well in position along Chickamauga Creek until 19 September. Bragg, having lost his golden opportunity to destroy the Federals in the passes, issued orders for an attack on the Federal left (north) flank at dawn on the 18th. This attack could have overwhelmed the Federals at that point, but it was frustrated by Union cavalry and never developed. Now Bragg and his generals had cooperated to lose a pretty collection of opportunities. But they still had their superior numbers of troops.

The night of the 18th, both sides prepared for battle, Rosecrans building a strong defensive position. Because of the thick woods in the area neither general knew where his enemy was – or, indeed, where his own forces were. Bragg thought the Union left was at Lee's and Gordon's Mill, and planned his attack to flank that position and gain the road to Chattanooga. Since Rosecrans had anticipated that, he had strung his lines out north from the mill and along the road. By daybreak on 19 September Thomas had formed his line of battle above the steep sides of Horseshoe Ridge.

Above: General Simon Bolivar Buckner CSA (1823-1914).

Left: On the road to Chickamauga, both armies left destruction of land and property behind.

The Battle of
Chickamauga began by
accident when cavalry
scouts of both armies met
on Reed's Bridge road.

As dawn came on the 19th, both armies were poised for battle at Chickamauga Creek. Prophetically, the creek's name came from an old Cherokee Indian word meaning 'River of Death.' A Union captain remembered the feelings of the men that morning:

Through that forenoon we saw the constantly moving columns of the enemy's infantry and saw battery after battery as they moved before us like a great panorama. In such moments men grow pale and lose their nerve. They are hungry, but they can not eat; they are tired, but they can not sit down. You speak to them, and they answer as if half asleep; they laugh, but the laugh has no joy in it.

The battle began by accident. Unsure whether there were Confederates north of the creek, Thomas sent cavalry to scout his front. Soon these men stumbled on some of Forrest's cavalrymen, who were dismounted on the Reed's Bridge road. The Southerners retreated under fire back to their infantry, who then pushed forward. Slowly the battle spread outward until both armies were firing all along the line. There followed a confused but nonetheless bloody day of fighting. As Hill late wrote, 'it was the sparring of the amateur boxer, and not the crushing blows of the trained pugilist.' All morning there was a gap of some two miles in the Federal lines, but it was hours before Bragg found the gap and tried to exploit it. Finally, an attempt was

Above: Confederate Cavalry attack a Federal supply train.

The river fog and the smoke from the cannon made visibility difficult for both sides.

made by the forces of John B Hood, whose division of Longstreet's command had just arrived ahead of the others. Hood smashed the right center of the Union line and got onto the Chattanooga road, but a wave of Federals charged in to drive them back. A Union soldier wrote of Hood's charge:

An artilleryman is shot down; a man from the infantry takes his place and obeys orders as best he can. When the charge begins our men are lying down. Now, in the midst of it, so great has become the excitement, so intense the anxiety, all fear and prudence vanishes, and the men leap to their feet, and fire and load, and fire and load, in the wildest frenzy of desperation. They have lost all ideas of danger or the strength of the

Above: The Confederate Infantry in the Chickamauga woods.

assailants. It was this absolute *desperation* of our men that held our lines.

After a day of heavy but indecisive fighting on 19 September the guns fell silent in the late afternoon. By then Longstreet had arrived by rail with the rest of his forces. It took him until 11 at night to find Bragg, who got out of bed for a conference. Dividing his army into two wings, Bragg gave the right to Polk and the left to Longstreet. Polk was to begin at dawn with a strong assault on Thomas; after Polk's attack there were to be successive attacks down the line to

the south. As the Confederate general spoke they heard the sound of axes from the Federal lines – the Army of the Cumberland was building a strong defensive line of log breastworks through the thick woods.

At dawn on the 20th visibility was negligible due to the woods and a thick blanket of fog. Bragg sat in his headquarters straining to hear the sound of Polk's dawn attack. After an hour of inactivity a messenger was dispatched to find Polk. The general was discovered reading a newspaper on a farmhouse porch whilst waiting for his breakfast. When queried

Above: By the end of the campaign the Confederates were reduced to hurling rocks at the enemy.

At the early stages of the
battle, the armies still
maintained their neat
ranks.

Above: Major General John Bell Hood CSA (1831-78).

Below: Hood had lost the use of his left arm at Gettysburg, but led his troops at Chickamauga until wounded in the right leg.

about his attack, Polk grandly responded, 'Do tell General Bragg that my heart is overflowing with anxiety for the attack – overflowing with anxiety, sir!' When this was reported at about nine-thirty to Bragg, he swore, 'in a manner that would have powerfully assisted a mule team in getting up a mountain,' and ordered the attack on Thomas begun immediately.

By this time the front stretched some two miles, north to south. Polk's men fell with a will onto Thomas, who held onto his breastworks in the Horseshoe Ridge but soon found his more vulnerable left flank being pushed across the vital road to Chattanooga. Again and again Thomas called for reinforcements from Rosecrans, to whom he had a direct telegraph wire (one of the first of these on any battlefield). Confusion began to creep into Union deployments due to the thick woods. At eleven in the morning this confusion created a strange and catastrophic turn in the battle. An aide, who had been riding behind the Union position, reported to Rosecrans that there was a gap in the Federal line between T J Wood's and J J Reynolds' division. Intending to seal that gap, Rosecrans hurriedly sent an order to Wood to move left, to 'close up on and support' Reynolds (both these corps lay near the Federal right flank, which was so far inactive).

But the aide had made a disastrous mistake: there was no gap in the Union line. Between Wood and Reynolds was John Brannan's division, exactly where they were supposed to be, but so hidden by the woods that the aide had not seen them. Thus the actual positions were Reynolds – Brannan – Wood.

Wood received Rosecrans' order and puzzled over it. How was he to 'close up on and support' Reynolds when Brannan was between them? Finally Wood decided that 'support' was the operative idea and ordered his division to pull out of line and march

behind Brannan toward Reynolds. His men formed line of march and headed for the rear, leaving a gaping hole in the Union right wing.

At just that moment, hardly a stone's throw away but still hidden in the woods, Longstreet was massing eight brigades for the attack. (That the attack was gathering then and there was apparently sheer coincidence.) At the head of the column rode hard-fighting John B Hood. About eleven-thirty in the morning the Confederates headed for the Union lines and found to their astonishment that no one was there.

The results were immediate and dramatic. A solid column of screaming Rebels flooded straight through the Union line, crashed onto the end of Wood's departing column and scattered the divisions of Federal generals Philip Sheridan and Jefferson C Davis, who had begun moving into the gap from the right. Hood, having lost the use of an arm at Gettysburg, was wounded seriously in the leg, but his men pushed on. At Rosecrans' headquarters an observer described an incredible sight:

I had not slept much for two nights and lay down on the grass. I was awakened by the most infernal noise I ever heard. I sat up, and the first thing I saw was General Rosecrans crossing himself – he was a very devout Catholic. 'Hello!' I said to myself. 'If the general is crossing himself, we are in a desperate situation.'
I looked around toward the front where all this din came from and I saw our lines break and melt away like leaves before the wind. Then the headquarters around me disappeared. The graybacks came through with a rush, and soon the musket balls and the cannon shot began to reach the place where we stood. The whole right of the army had apparently been routed.

From the other side, a Southern soldier remembered that exhilarating charge:

Short and bloody was the work. We moved steadily forward, no halting. The men rushed over the hastily constructed breastworks of logs and rails of the foe, with the old-time familiar Rebel yell. Wheeling to the right, the column swept before it and pushed along the Chattanooga road toward Missionary Ridge in pursuit. It was glorious!'

During this rout the Federals lost thousands in casualties and captured; Hill later wrote that he had never seen Federal dead so thickly blanketing the ground except after the suicidal charge at Fredericksburg. Among the fleeing were a panicky and demoralized Rosecrans and most of his staff. Assuming his whole army was routed, Rosecrans ordered everyone to retreat to Chattanooga.

Fortunately for the Union, not everyone obeyed that order, because Rosecrans was wrong about his forces being totally routed. Along Horseshoe Ridge

to the left, Thomas was holding on like grim death, with thousands of enemy swarming around the steep sides of the ridge. At Confederate headquarters Longstreet was begging General Bragg to give him all his remaining troops to surround Thomas's position. Bragg, seemingly of the opinion that his army was losing, replied that the rest of the men had 'no fight left in them.' Having fought at the side of Lee most of the war, Longstreet's frustration with the obtuse Bragg must have been titanic.

By mid-afternoon Thomas was watching enemy forces moving toward his right. He knew his front along the precipitous slopes was strong, but his flanks were in great danger. But not all the routed Federal divisions had continued on to Chattanooga. Wood, Brannan and Reynolds fell into position on Thomas's right Wood meeting the first appearance of Longstreet's men with a determined bayonet charge that stopped the Rebels in their tracks. As Thomas's line on the right stabilized a little, Rebel assaults swarmed onto his left flank. D H Hill later wrote admiringly of Thomas's stand, 'that indomitable Virginia soldier, George H Thomas, was there and was destined to save the Union army from total rout and ruin, by confronting with invincible pluck the forces of his friend and captain in the Mexican War.'

As the afternoon wore on Thomas's Federals were running out of ammunition, their front and flanks were staggering under heavy assaults, the enemy was moving around the right flank to the rear. Rebel cannons were moving into position to enfilade the Union right and there were no men left to do anything about it. And then at three-thirty the final blow seemed at hand Thomas noticed a column of dust approaching in his rear. If that column were foe, his men were doomed. An officer was dispatched to take a look. They proved to be friends, part of two divisions of reserves commanded by General Gordon Granger, who had just committed a serious and most salutary breach of orders. Placed in reserve by Rosecrans with strict orders to guard the road to Chattanooga, Granger had listened with increasing anxiety to the sound of battle growing steadily on the Federal left. Finally, he made his own decision – 'I am going to Thomas, orders or no orders.' By four o'clock Granger was shaking hands with an overjoyed Thomas, men and ammunition arriving rapidly behind him. Granger's men cleared the enemy from a valley in the rear, and a path of retreat was clear.

Orders came from Rosecrans to retreat, but Thomas was determined to hold out until dark. Ammunition was running low again; about six o'clock another Rebel charge on the left was turned back with bayonets. But at last dark came and Thomas withdrew his troops to Chattanooga. Behind him the exhausted Confederates finally placed their banner on the summit.

The South had won the field at Chickamauga. However accidental the victory, it was one of the greatest of the war in the Western Theater. But General George Thomas had saved the Federal army to fight another day, becoming in the process one of the immortal heroes of the Union cause. To history, Thomas is forever 'The Rock of Chickamauga.'

Hooker's forces attack Lookout Mountain, Tennessee.

Right: Grant and his staff survey Lookout Mountain after the battle.

Casualties in the battle were among the worst of the war: of 66,326 Southerners engaged, there were 2312 killed, 14,674 wounded, 1468 missing, a total of 18,454 casualties; for the North, of 58,222 engaged, there were 1657 killed, 9756 wounded, 4757 missing, a total of 16,170. Altogether, nearly 35,000 men fell; both sides had lost 28 percent of their forces.

Back in his headquarters, Bragg could not seem to get it into his head that he had won. His generals pressed him to pursue, the impetuous Forrest screaming at his commander, 'You are a coward and a damned scoundrel!' By next morning, 21 September, Bragg was finally willing to admit victory. He sent a force to Missionary Ridge in Chattanooga with orders to attack; but Bragg's men found the Federals 'ready to receive and entertain us.' A Confederate commentator summarized. 'At the close of the battle we could have strolled into Chattanooga; now it was vigorously defended. This was the fruit of the great battle, the pitiable end of the glorious victory that was ours.'

Yet Bragg had one more chance to reclaim Chattanooga. He put is army in strong position on the ridges and settled in to starve the Yankees out. The Federal army was now besieged deep in enemy territory. And starve the Yankees did, while both Bragg and Rosecrans spent their time writing elaborate reports blaming their subordinates for everything.

On 23 October, 1863, General Ulysses S Grant arrived in Chattanooga. He had been appointed to command of most Union forces west of the Alleghenies. His first act was to replace the spent Rosecrans with Thomas as commander of the Army of the Cumberland. Gaining reinforcements, Grant soon had food and supplies flowing into the city. And on 25 December the vindictive Federals, shouting 'Chickamauga!' as they charged, swarmed up and over the slopes of Missionary Ridge and chased the Confederate Army of Tennessee back to Georgia in one of the worst routs the Confederacy ever suffered. Chattanooga, the strategic center of the South, was secure for the Union. Now the Confederacy was squeezed into a narrow band of coastal states, and the way was prepared for William Tecumseh Sherman's devastating march across Georgia to the sea.

Contemplating this last golden opportunity lost, General D H Hill later concluded:

Below: General John Pope USA (1823-92).

It seems to me that the *èlan* of the Southern soldier was never seen after Chickamauga – that brilliant dash which had distinguished him was gone forever. He was too intelligent not to know that the cutting in two of Georgia meant death to all his hopes ... He fought stoutly to the last, but, after Chickamauga, with the sullenness of despair and without the enthusiasm of hope. That 'barren victory' sealed the fate of the Southern Confederacy.

CHAPTER X

SPOTSYLVANIA

Previous spread: At Spotsylvania, the armies met on ground they had fought over the year before.

Below: The Confederate position at Spotsylvania was surrounded by entrenchments.

On 4 May 1864, the Union Army of the Potomac pulled out of Culpeper, Virginia, and once again headed for Richmond. The army was stronger than ever, with 122,000 men newly organized into three corps. Nonetheless, the troops were considerably more cynical about their prospects than during General McClellan's abortive 'On to Richmond' campaign of 1862. They had seen commanders come and go with great frequency over the course of their campaigns against Robert E Lee. They had little faith that the new man would fare any better.

The new man was General Ulysses S Grant, whom President Lincoln had just named to head the entire Union war effort. Grant had immediately produced a plan characteristic of him: a five-pronged offensive involving a complex series of operations over all the theaters of the war. Three of those campaigns were unsuccessful; the other two, William Tecumseh Sherman's march through Georgia and Grant's campaign against the Army of Northern Virginia, were to prove sufficient to end the war – but only after another agonizing year of fighting.

Grant and the Army of the Potomac (General Meade was still nominally in command, but Grant rode with the army) crossed the Rapidan and headed southeast across Virginia on the most direct road to Richmond. Grant knew that somewhere on that road Lee would be waiting for him, his army ragged and gaunt with hunger but still dangerous. In two columns the Federals marched nervously into the Wilderness, scene of their humiliation the year before in the battle of Chancellorsville. As Hooker had tried to do, Grant wanted to get his forces out of that jungle and into the open.

Then Grant got his first lesson about Robert E Lee: the Southern commander did not cotton to letting his enemy choose the time and place to fight. With his army at just over half the strength of the Federals, Lee pounced on Grant's column in the Wilderness. In the two days of fierce and confused fighting that ensued on 5 and 6 May, there was a near-repeat of Chancellorsville. The Federals were outfought and out-generaled; by the end of the second day Longstreet's men were rolling up the Federal lines. During the fighting Grant had a crisis of confidence much like Joe Hooker's, and was seen

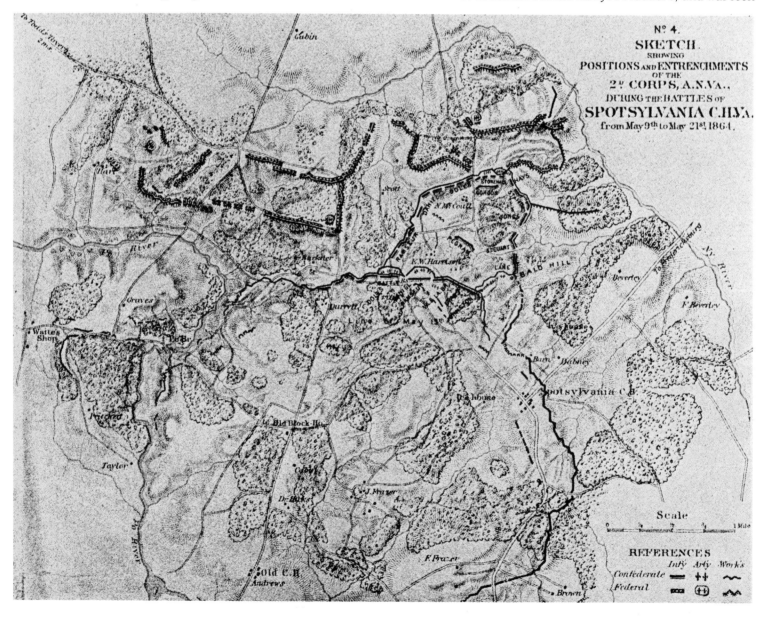

sobbing in his tent. Unlike Hooker, Grant soon recovered the cold bulldog tenacity that had made him victorious. Nonetheless, disaster loomed for the Union in the Wilderness until fate stepped in – Longstreet was seriously wounded by his own men (not five miles from where Stonewall Jackson had met the same accident a year before). Longstreet survived, but was out of commission. The Southern attack faltered and both armies sank to a standstill. Losses were already worse for the Union than at Antietam – 17,666 casualties; Southern casualties were uncounted, but probably less than half that figure.

It had been Longstreet who had warned his peers about Grant: 'That man will fight us every day and every hour till the end of the war.' Longstreet proved accurate. After the battle in the Wilderness the Confederates expected their enemy to retreat as usual, but Lee also knew his man, and knew better. To General John B Gordon Lee observed, 'General Grant is not going to retreat. He will move his army to Spotsylvania. I am so sure of his next move that I have already made arrangements . . . to meet him there.'

Lee was right. On the night of 7 May Grant shifted his forces around Lee's right flank and moved toward Spotsylvania – like Chancellorsville, another insignificant road crossing on the way to Richmond. The Federals began their march angrily, supposing they were 'on another skedaddle.' Then at a road crossing they found their advance turning south, not north. Wild cheers broke out from the men of the North as Grant rode to the head of the column. At last they had a general who would let them fight.

However, the Federals were going to have to fight before they expected to – Lee's forces were moving parallel to them in a desperate race to the crossroads. At dawn on 8 May the Federal advance reached the road between Todd's Tavern and Spotsylvania; to their astonishment they found the enemy waiting

Above: General in Chief of the Armies of the United States Ulysses Simpson Grant (1822-85) preferred commanding in the field.

Left: The Union Army camped at Spotsylvania.

spent entrenching. Lee's lines took shape east to west where they had fallen in the fighting of 8 May. The result on the Southern side was a large, irregular crescent along the higher ground, in the middle of which was a large, bulging salient which at that time was dubbed the 'mule shoe.' History would remember it, however, with the name earned by a kink in the salient's line: 'Bloody Angle.'

On the morning of the 10th Lee discovered a Federal move on his left and dispatched Heth and Early, who drove the Yankees back across the Po River with heavy losses. In midafternoon another Union assault met a bloody repulse to the left of the Confederate salient.

Just before dusk, however, there was a more significant development. A young colonel named Emory Upton persuaded Grant to let him have a try at the 'mule shoe.' Gathering 12 infantry regiments, with reinforcements on the way, Upton led a solid column toward the northwest face of the salient.

The toughest fight yet – A. R. Waud

Above: Federal troops crouch in a captured trench near the salient.

Right: JEB Stuart was killed in the battle at Yellow Tavern.

Below: The Union force attacked the salient, but were repulsed.

for them. It was cavalry under Fitzhugh Lee, Robert's nephew. The South had won the race. Fitzhugh Lee was soon reinforced and repulsed three feeble charges by the exhausted Federals.

When he came from Tennessee, Grant had brought with him to head his cavalry a short, feisty young general named Philip Sheridan. He was to become a legend of the war, but at this point Sheridan was new and an upstart. That day in the midst of a violent quarrel with Meade concerning who got in whose way on the march to Spotsylvania, Sheridan boasted he could whip Jeb Stuart. Hearing of this, Grant replied, 'Sheridan generally knows what he's talking about,' and let him go. Sheridan and the Union cavalry was ordered out – and good riddance, as far as Meade was concerned – on a raid toward Richmond, which Stuart would be obliged to contest.

On 9 May there was skirmishing between the armies at Spotsylvania, but most of the time was

They discovered the Rebels had fashioned a formidable position – a trench fronted by banked logs, with a headlog on top leaving space to fire beneath; in front of this parapet was a solid tangle of abatis – felled trees with sharpened limbs.

Upton's men charged across open ground straight at the Southern line. At once a hail of bullets tore into them. The Federal soldiers in front fell in dozens, but somehow a spearhead got through the abatis to the parapet and began firing, clubbing and stabbing into the Rebels in the trench behind, some of the Yankees pitching their bayoneted rifles in like harpoons. Somehow, it worked: the Federals smashed through the strongest part of the Confederate line. All they needed now were more troops and they could break Lee's army. But Union reinforcements were stopped by a wall of Southern artillery fire, and Rebel reinforcements began appearing in force. Upton soon found himself out on a limb and pulled back with heavy losses – taking

with him some 1000 prisoners. His charge had failed, but he had proved the salient was vulnerable. 'A brigade today – we'll try a corps tomorrow,' Grant said. He picked Winfield Scott Hancock, his most dynamic general and the hero of Gettysburg, to take the battle-honed II Corps down to assault the salient.

But Federal troop movements and rainy weather delayed the assault for a day. There were two events of note that 11 May, however. That day Grant sent a defiant telegram to Washington, proclaiming, 'I propose to fight it out on this line if it takes all summer.' And over to the east, Sheridan got his crack at Jeb Stuart.

In a battle between the opposing cavalries at Yellow Tavern, things were going badly for the Rebel Horsemen. Stuart was directing his forces when a Federal private got a bead on him at ten yards. The gallant Cavalier had led his last raid; he went down, mortally wounded at the age of 31. Jeb Stuart's death ended a legendary career in the Southern army, and ended as well the cavalry superiority that had been a major ingredient in Lee's success. Though Sheridan's further campaign toward Richmond came to little, he had bagged a very big prize indeed.

At Spotsylvania, dawn approached on 12 May, promising a sullen foggy and drizzly morning.

Confederate general Edward Johnson awoke early and inspected his position at the head of the salient. He was worried, very worried. Salients were dangerous, especially when held by infantry alone, because the arc of the salient created a diverging offensive fire while it made for a converging fire by the enemy. Salients were workable artillery positions, though – guns could be posted to sweep the sides of the angle and enfilade attackers.

What worried Johnson most was that the night before Lee had taken away the salient's cannons, its only security, to meet a supposed Federal threat on the right. Johnson was certain that the real attack was gathering on his front. He had urgently asked for the cannons to be returned, and Lee had agreed. But here was dawn, and the cannons were not back. Johnson knew that behind him new breastworks were being built across the base of the salient for a withdrawal, but they were far from being completed. Then Johnson heard something.

He strained to listen in the wet, heavy air. It was cheering in the distance, a jumble of cheering and shouting voices moving toward him. But if it was the attack, why were his pickets not firing? Had they been swallowed in the enemy advance? Johnson glanced back: still no cannons. His men, 5000 strong, awoke and stood to their posts, listening. He peered forward again. Then out of the fog, directly

Above: The Confederates captured a Union breastworks.

Below: The Union Army had learned the value of 'total warfare.'

Inexorably, it rolled onto and over the breastworks. Just before he was captured, Johnson saw his 20 cannons arriving at a gallop, but the Federal advance simply swallowed them up.

To the rear, behind his incomplete breastworks at the base of the salient, Robert E Lee sat on his horse and listened. He had heard what happened – a furious burst of fire, then an ominous silence, a silence of utter catastrophe: the Federals had broken through his line and now they were using the bayonet on his men. A broken line could not be held. His army was dying in that silence and haze out there.

Lee spurred his horse over to where his reserves lay, the division of General John B Gordon. If Gordon's men could hold off the attack until the new breastworks were ready, the army had a chance. When Lee galloped up Gordon was already moving to the attack. Seeing this, Lee wheeled and headed for the front of the column. The implication was clear: at this moment of supreme danger Lee intended to head the attack himself. He would lead them to victory or die in the attempt.

Suddenly Gordon's mount was in front of Lee. Gordon was seizing the bridle of Lee's horse and

before his works, rolled a solid wall of blue-clad figures.

The Confederate position erupted into flame, but the hail of bullets could not stop Hancock's 20,000 men. As the Federals in front fell, the human wave rolled over them and trampled them into the mud.

shouting, 'General Lee, you shall not lead my men. They have never failed you. They will not fail you now!' Soldiers gathered around the two generals; a mumble grew out of them that rose to a cadenced shout: 'General Lee to the rear!' General Lee to the rear!' He was their best hope, they would not risk his life. The men seemed almost bodily to pick up Lee and his horse and shove them back. Helpless, Lee gave in and rode to the rear, turning to shout, 'God bless the Virginians!' as the men charged out toward the Federals in the salient. Along with Gordon the divisions of Rodes and Ramseur fell like a thunderclap on the disorganized Yankees and herded them back over the breastworks.

But there the Federals stayed. They had been routed too many times. Now they had a general who would let them fight and the numbers to win, and they were not going to retreat again. For the Southerners there was an equally simple equation: the line must be held or everything had been in vain, all the suffering and dying. The line must hold or the war was lost.

So on a line a mile wide two armies concentrated their full might upon the two sides of the same parapet, and the result was a day-long, hand-to-hand melee of horrifying savagery. It was suicide to stay for long at that place, but men stayed nonetheless, shooting and stabbing over the breastworks and under the headlogs until they died. They became crazed, like sharks in frenzy. They stood and fired until they dropped and their bodies were trampled and shot to pieces. Rain poured down, and the trenches ran with water and blood and flesh, and men in their thirst drank of it. Cannons were run into the breastworks to spray canister directly into the living and dying and dead a few yards away – artillery charging infantry in a mad inversion. They fired until their crew and carriages were shot away.

At times a soldier would leap onto the breastworks and fire into the enemy, his mates handing him loaded guns, until he was shot down and someone else leaped up. Over the screams and curses a deep humming sound writhed over Bloody Angle; it was the sound of tens of thousands of bullets. In the history of the world there had never been such concentrated gunfire at such close range. The breastworks dissolved into splinters; behind the line large trees were shattered and felled by musket fire (one of the reasons anyone at all could survive was that most were shooting too high). Fighting like

Below: Many wounded died when flames engulfed the Wilderness.

demons, the soldiers began to resemble demons as well: their faces black with gunpowder and twisted with agony and rage, their bodies splashed with blood, they screamed and cursed and growled. It was a collective insanity of indescribable horror.

The nightmare lasted some 20 hours. The only lulls had come when both sides stopped firing to throw the dead out of the trenches – the bodies impeded the fighting. Other Federal attacks on both sides of the salient failed during the day. At three o'clock in the morning there was silence at last on Bloody Angle. The Confederates pulled back to the completed breastworks at the base of the salient and the Federals claimed the ghastly parapet and its chest-high heaps of dead and wounded. The Confederate line still held as strongly as ever. Nearly

Right: With Lee's surrender, many Confederate officers returned to Richmond to give themselves up.

Below: The Army of Tennessee under Joseph Johnston was the last major Confederate Force to surrender.

seven thousand Northerners had fallen, and probably more Southerners, for that now utterly useless square mile of land.

The battle continued for another seven days, with an abortive major Federal offensive on the 18th, but its fury was spent. Grant slowly slipped his army toward Lee's right, and on 19 May again tried to run around his enemy toward Richmond. Again Lee anticipated the move, again won the race. The final convulsion of that terrible campaign came at Cold Harbor, near Richmond, on 3 June. There Grant sent a huge and horrifyingly stupid frontal attack onto Lee's entrenchments; during it the North lost some 7000 casualties in 20 minutes, to no purpose whatever. As one observer noted, the Army of the Potomac had 'literally marched in blood and agony

from the Rapidan to the James.' For one month the survivors had marched, slept and fought a continuous battle in the same sweat- and blood-stiffened uniforms. There had been 50,000 Union casualties, averaging some 2000 per day, amounting to 41 percent of the original forces. The South had lost 32,000, 46 percent, and these losses, unlike the North's, were irreplaceable.

Grant had proclaimed he would fight it out all summer, but finally had to face the galling truth: even with twice the men he could not beat Robert E Lee on the field. Grant had tried to bludgeon his enemy to death and had failed, because his own army could no longer endure it.

On 7 June Grant issued new orders. Richmond lay to the west, but the Army of the Potomac marched south. Now Grant was going to take the only course he had that promised sure success. He would besiege Petersburg, which was Richmond's only line to the outside, and drain the lifeblood of Lee's army if necessary by one drop at a time.

There were no great battles left to the Confederacy now, only the slow agony of failing strength and hope in the trenches of Petersburg. On 2 April 1865, after six months of devastating siege, Lee and the remains of his army bolted from Petersburg. Lee was making a last desperate effort to join forces with Joseph E Johnston's army in South Carolina; his leaving doomed Richmond. But Lee was run

aground by Grant and Sheridan, who circled and harried the pathetic remains of the Army of Northern Virginia until that 9 April at Appomattox, when Lee's men made their last charge, breaking through the center of Sheridan's line as it blocked their path. For a brief moment there was open country in front of the Army of Northern Virginia. Then from over a hill appeared Union infantry, line after line of blue marching to fill that last gateway to freedom. Then from within Confederate lines came a rider carrying a white flag into the ranks of the enemy.

The war was over, and it was not over. Lee's surrender to Grant at Appomattox on 9 April 1865, largely ended the hostilities (Johnston surrendered to Sherman on the 18th). Now the country was one again, the glorious exploits of the men in gray a matter for history and for pride. But the assassination of Lincoln on 14 April was only the first of the war's aftershocks that would never leave the consciousness of the nation.

Throughout the long days of the war a volunteer nurse in Union military hospitals had put into impassioned words his thoughts about the struggle. He was Walt Whitman, later to be recognized as the great poet of the reborn nation. At the war's conclusion, Whitman wrote this benediction:

The dead in this war – there they lie, strewing the

fields and woods and valleys and battlefields of the South: Virginia, the Peninsula, Malvern Hill and Fair Oaks, the banks of the Chickahominy, the terraces of Fredericksburg, Antietam bridge, the grisly ravines of Manassas, the bloody promenade of the Wilderness.

The dead, the dead, the dead . . . somewhere they crawled to die, alone, in bushes, low gullies, or on the sides of hills . . . Our young men once so handsome and so joyous, taken from us . . . the clusters of camp graves . . . the single graves left in the woods or by the roadside . . . the general million, and the special cemeteries in almost all the states.

The infinite dead, the land entire saturated, perfumed with their impalpable ashes' exhalation in Nature's chemistry distilled; and shall be so forever, in every future grain of wheat and ear of corn, and every flower that grows, and every breath we draw.

Below: General Robert E Lee, with his son Rooney and nephew Fitzhugh, at the end of the war.

INDEX

Page numbers in italics refer to illustrations

ACKNOWLEDGMENTS

The publisher would like to thank the following people who have helped in the preparation of this book: Ron Callow, who designed it; Elizabeth M Montgomery, who edited it; Mary R Raho and Shiela Byrd, who did the picture research; Florence Norton, who prepared the index.

PICTURE CREDITS

Raymond Baylees: 60 (top).
Bison Picture Library: 18-19, 23, 24 (top), 30-31, 53 (bottom left), 65 (bottom), 84-85, 88 (bottom), 102-103, 137 (bottom), 142-143, 170-171.
Bowdoin College: 150 (bottom)
Anne S K Brown Military Collection: 11 (bottom left), 26, 27 (top right), 40-41, 46 (top), 50, 53 (top), 68 (left), 86, 88 (top), 89 (top), 124, 132 (top), 134-135, 138-139, 141 (top), 151, 152 (top), 176 (bottom), 180-181, 182, 184 (middle), 185.
Chicago Historical Society: 11 (bottom right), 56-57, 60 (bottom), 70 (right), 75 (top), 76 (bottom), 77 (top), 107, 148-149, 156-15 ?, 160-161, 178, 179.
Rutherford B Hayes Presidential Center; 24 (bottom), 27 (bottom right), 28 (bottom), 29 (top), 30 (top), 44, 48 (bottom), 53 (bottom right), 61 (top), 70 (left), 90 (top), 94 (bottom), 106 (left), 112 (bottom), 158, 173 (top), 186 (top).
S E King: 2-3, 73, 80-81, 94 (top), 114 (top), 120-121, 130.
Kurz & Allison: 174-175.
Library of Congress: 4-5, 6-7, 8 (top and bottom), 9 (top), 10 (bottom), 11 (top right and left), 12 (top and bottom), 16, 17 (top and bottom), 20, 21 (top and bottom), 29 (bottom right), 32-33, 34 (bottom), 35 (bottom), 37, 38-39, 42-43, 46 (bottom), 47, 48 (top), 49 (top and bottom), 51 (top and bottom), 52, 55, 58, 59 (bottom), 61 (bottom), 66-67, 69, 71 (top), 72 (top and bottom), 74-75, 78, 82 (top and bottom),

90 bottom, 96-97, 10, 105, 114 (bottom), 117, 122, 125, 126-127, 128, 131 (right), 132 (bottom), 133, 136 (left), 140, 144 (left), 145, 146, 147 (top), 150 (top), 153, 154, 155, 159, 162 (top and bottom), 166 (top), 167, 169 (top), 173 (top), 176 (top), 183 (bottom), 184 (top), 186 (bottom), 187, 188 (top and bottom), 189, 190.
The Mansell Collection: 168 (top).
Museum of the Confederacy: 14 (top), 45, 54, 72 (middle), 87, 92-93, 101, 110-111, 116.
National Archives: 9 (bottom), 35 (top), 63, 183 (top).
Richard Natkiel: 10 (top), 22 (both), 71 (bottom).
Naval History: 34 (top), 59 (top), 68 (right).
Naval Photographic Center: 62, 65 (top and middle).
New York Public Library: 13 (top), 14 (bottom), 15, 36, 77 (bottom), .79, 83, 91 (top and bottom), 95, 98, 99 (top and bottom), 104, 108-109, 112 (top), 113, 115 (both), 118, 129, 131 (left), 141 (both), 144 (right), 147 (bottom), 166 (bottom), 168 (bottom), 169 (bottom), 172 (bottom), 177, 184 (bottom).
Peter Newark's Western Americana: 1, 29 (bottom left), 41 (top), 76 (top), 106 (right), 119, 123, 136 (right), 137 (top and middle), 152 (bottom), 172 (top).
Smithsonian Institution: 163.
VMI Museum: 25, 28 (top), 89 (bottom), 164-165.
Virginia State Library: 64.